# BEHAVIORAL SCIENCE AND THE SECRET SERVICE: Toward the Prevention of Assassination

Division of Mental Health
and Behavioral Medicine
INSTITUTE OF MEDICINE

Jane Takeuchi
Fredric Solomon
W. Walter Menninger
*Editors*

NATIONAL ACADEMY PRESS
Washington, D.C.    1981

<u>IOM</u>

The Institute of Medicine was chartered in 1970 by the National Academy of Sciences to enlist distinguished members of the appropriate professions in the examination of policy matters pertaining to the health of the public. In this, the Institute acts under both the Academy's 1863 congressional charter responsibility to be an adviser to the federal government and its own initiative in identifying issues of medical care, research, and education.

This conference summary was developed by the staff of the Division of Mental Health and Behavioral Medicine, Institute of Medicine, with the advice and assistance of the planning committee chairman, W. Walter Menninger. Conclusions and recommendations by conference participants on matters of policy are reported to assure completeness of the summary, but are not recommendations of the Institute of Medicine.

IOM Publication Number 81-008

Library of Congress Catalog Card Number 81-85235

International Standard Book Number 0-309-03225-3

*Available from*
National Academy Press
2101 Constitution Avenue, N.W.
Washington, D.C. 20418

Printed in the United States of America

National Academy of Sciences

Institute of Medicine Workshop on Behavioral Research and the
Secret Service: Problems in Assessing and Managing
Dangerous Behavior

Planning Committee

W. Walter Menninger, M.D., Chair*
Senior Staff Psychiatrist
Division of Law and Psychiatry
Menninger Foundation
Topeka, KS

Elissa P. Benedek, M.D.
Director
Center for Forensic Psychiatry
Ann Arbor, MI

Joseph T. English, M.D.*
Director of Psychiatry
St. Vincent's Hospital
New York, NY

Shervert H. Frazier, M.D.
Psychiatrist-in-Chief
McLean Hospital
Belmont, MA

David A. Hamburg, M.D.*
Director
Division of Health Policy
  Research and Education
Harvard University
Cambridge, MA

Kenneth R. Hammond, Ph.D.
Professor of Psychology
Center for Research
  on Judgment and Policy
Institute of Behavioral Sciences
University of Colorado
Boulder, CO

Lincoln E. Moses, Ph.D.*
Professor
Department of Statistics
Stanford University
Stanford, CA

Frank M. Ochberg, M.D.
Director
Department of Mental Health
State of Michigan
Lansing, MI

Saleem A. Shah, Ph.D.
Chief
Center for Studies of Crime
  and Delinquency
National Institute of Mental
  Health
Rockville, MD

Alan A. Stone, M.D.
Professor of Law and
  Psychiatry
Center for Advanced Study
  in the Behavioral Sciences
Stanford, CA

Charles H. Whitebread, L.L.B.
Visiting Professor of Law
University of Southern
  California Law Center
University Park
Los Angeles, CA

*Member, Institute of Medicine

Marvin E. Wolfgang, Ph.D.
Professor of Sociology and
    Professor of Law
University of Pennsylvania
Center for Studies in
    Criminology and
    Criminal Law
Philadelphia, PA

Franklin E. Zimring, J.D.
Professor of Law
University of Chicago
    Law School
Chicago, IL

Workshop Staff

Jane Takeuchi, Ph.D.
Staff Officer
Division of Mental Health and
    Behavioral Medicine

Delores Parron, Ph.D.
Associate Director
Division of Mental Health and
    Behavioral Medicine

Fredric Solomon, M.D.
Director
Division of Mental Health and
    Behavioral Medicine

Mireille Mesias
Secretary
Division of Mental Health and
    Behavioral Medicine

# CONTENTS

# INTRODUCTION AND OVERVIEW

W. Walter Menninger, M.D.
Conference Chair

No act is more repugnant or more upsetting to a democratic system of government than presidential assassination. During the 205 years of this Republic, one of every four presidents has been the target of an assassin's bullet. This traumatic event was again experienced by the American people last March 30 with the shooting of President Ronald Reagan as he left a speaking engagement at a Washington hotel.

Charged with the protection of the president, the United States Secret Service has an enormous responsibility, a responsibility that is increasingly difficult to fulfill in our individualistic, mobile, affluent, gun-prevalent society. Ever since the assassinations of President John F. Kennedy in 1963 and his presidential-candidate brother Robert in 1968, there have been searching studies of the phenomenon of assassination and how to protect presidents and presidential candidates from such attacks. One such study, a staff report prepared for the National Commission on the Causes and Prevention of Violence, concluded:

> We are as yet unable to comprehend the individual
> and social forces at work sufficiently to be able to
> identify potential assassins in advance of their
> attacks. Characteristics common to assassins are
> shared by a large number of citizens. It is,
> however, both impossible at this point and probably
> undesirable in a democratic political system to
> attempt to identify and isolate potential assassins
> on any broad scale based on present knowledge.*

Because of the problems cited by that Commission's staff, the Secret Service has invested heavily in assuring the adequate physical

---

*J. F. Kirkham, S. Levy, and W. J. Crotty, Assassination and Political Violence, A Staff Report to the National Commission on the Causes and Prevention of Violence (Washington, D. C.: U. S. Government Printing Office, 1969), p. xviii.

protection for the president and minimizing his exposure to risk. At the same time, the Secret Service is constantly confronted with a myriad of threats against the president and other persons whom it is mandated to protect. The Service is obligated to assess and respond both to known threats and unknown dangers to those it protects, as best it can. It fully recognizes a need to increase its capacity to assess and deal with threatening persons.

Approximately a year ago, following discussions initiated by the director of the Secret Service, H. S. Knight, and then-president of the Institute of Medicine of the National Academy of Sciences, David A. Hamburg, it was decided to convene a conference of behavioral scientists and clinicians to review some of the concerns of the Secret Service and explore ways behavioral science might help the Secret Service better cope with persons who threaten the president. In November 1980, after orientation by the Secret Service, a planning committee met to develop a conference agenda and to identify conference participants. Ultimately, 27 behavioral scientists met March 8 - 10, 1981, in Washington, D. C., for the formal conference. This group represented both clinical and research perspectives and included psychiatrists, psychologists, lawyers, decision theorists, and criminologists, along with staff from the Secret Service and the Institute of Medicine.

Prior to the conference, the invitees were briefed in depth about the mission and procedures of the Secret Service. The conference agenda itself was designed to expose the participants further to practical case problems encountered by the Secret Service. Formal papers and presentations explored issues and problems in assessing dangerous behavior and managing persons who threaten those protected by the Service. In plenary and small group workshops, the conferees considered a list of specific questions previously prepared by the Secret Service—ranging from indicators of dangerousness and the relationship of the Service to the mental health professions to what kind of research capacity the Service should develop. (A synopsis of the conference responses to those questions is appended herewith.)

As evidenced by its wholehearted support and participation, the Secret Service, and particularly its Intelligence Division, clearly wishes to learn from the behavioral science field all it can to improve its capacity to protect the president and others. Primarily action-oriented, the Service devotes most of its resources and energies to its day-to-day operations; it has little opportunity to reflect on, analyze, or evaluate some of its practices regarding the identification, assessment, and management of potential threateners. The Secret Service record-keeping and computer files emphasize actions taken rather than a comprehensive cataloguing of information that might provide a base for research and management information feedback. Not only is there a lack of standardized reporting for such things as the psychiatric and criminal history of threateners, but the research capacity of the Service is extremely limited, restricting its ability to learn from its experience and to determine whether its agents are operating consistently in the most efficient and effective manner.

From a review of the Secret Service caseload, it is evident that the Secret Service protection effort is preoccupied with a high percentage of persons with a history of mental illness, i.e., a known history of psychiatric in-patient or out-patient care. Only 10 percent of the Service's regularly-followed population of threateners has no history of mental illness. Although the attention of the Secret Service is focused on persons because of an acute threat made against the president, the threatener's behavior often reflects a chronic emotional disturbance for which the person is not receiving professional attention. While the Service must devote a great deal of energy to the evaluation and follow-up investigation of these emotionally troubled persons, the relationship between the Service and mental health service providers has been less than ideal. As a result, the Secret Service has not always been able to determine whether a given subject has actually received adequate evaluation and/or treatment for his or her emotional problems.

The conferees addressed issues of dangerousness and the limits in the prediction of dangerousness, management of dangerous persons, legal and ethical aspects of managing threatening persons, improving relationships between the Secret Service and the mental health community, research opportunities to improve Secret Service operations, and Secret Service agent training and selection—discussions that are detailed later in this report. The conferees also touched upon larger social issues, which are not under the control of the Secret Service but which nonetheless play a role in assassination: risk-taking behavior by the president or others protected by the Secret Service; the availability of the handgun as the concealable weapon of assassination; the current political climate, which is marked by polarized, highly emotional, single-issue antagonists who may express their extremism in violent confrontation; the repercussions of governmental cutbacks which may produce embittered, aggrieved persons who blame the president for their misfortune. There was a sense of urgency expressed that these were times when the president would be at greater risk and when the Secret Service should get all the help it could from the scientific community. Little did the conferees anticipate that but three weeks later the Secret Service protection would be breached.

This conference was a beginning. It did not produce any startling new insights, but there was identification of areas which merit further consultation and exploration. There was a consensus that what was started here should not end here. The conferees were not pressed to make any formal recommendations, and this report reflects areas of consensus and diversity of the participants' views.  Nonetheless, from my personal vantage point, I would urge consideration of the following:

By the Secret Service:
- establishing a behavioral science research advisory group to assist in the development of a practical and meaningful research program
- developing an interview format that will enable better data collection and provide a basis for retrospective and prospective study of threateners of persons protected by the Secret Service
- conducting a detailed analysis of how agents now make their decisions about threateners
- developing a training experience for agents that includes supervised interviewing of mentally ill persons
- developing a relationship with mental health agencies and practitioners of recognized quality, from whom the Secret Service can obtain consultation and assistance in assessing mentally ill subjects and interpreting clinical reports.

By the Institute of Medicine:
- supporting the efforts of the Secret Service to develop an effective research capacity
- facilitating the efforts of the Service to establish contact with recognized specialists in behavioral science research and clinical psychiatric practice and education.

By mental health practitioners:
- discussing in their professional associations the clinical and ethical dilemmas involved in their duty to protect the president, when caring for a patient who has made threats against the president as part of his or her illness.

In addition it is clear that the task of the Secret Service is complicated by other serious ongoing problems, the solutions for which lie beyond its scope.  Discussed in this conference were two problems that were considered at some length 12 years ago by the National Commission on the Causes and Prevention of Violence, of which I was a member.  First, the president and others protected by the Secret Service can either respect or disregard the limited capacity of the Secret Service to protect them.  To the extent that they take unnecessary risks as they fulfill their responsibilities, the capability of the Service to safeguard them is diminished. Second, with regard to the elements in our society which contribute to assassination, I am again impressed--as was the Violence

4

Commission--with the significant risk presented by the easy access to the primary instrument of assassination, the concealable handgun. It behooves our society to consider better ways to deal with this problem.

* * * * * * * * * *

This conference and resultant summary are the product of a substantial effort and commitment of a great many distinguished behavioral scientists who volunteered their time and energy in planning, preparing papers, and participating in the conference. All these persons deserve special thanks for their willingness to give of their knowledge and experience in an effort to enhance the work of the Secret Service in protecting our country's leaders.

In addition, the success of this effort also reflects the dedication and contributions of special agent Robert Kyanko who provided primary liason with the Secret Service; and Fredric Solomon, Director of the IOM Division of Mental Health and Behavioral Medicine; Jane Takeuchi, IOM staff officer; and Mireille Mesias, administrative secretary. I am particularly appreciative of the work of Dr. Takeuchi in reviewing the lengthy conference transcripts to prepare the initial draft of the detailed, integrated summary of workshop and plenary discussions.

QUESTIONS RAISED BY THE SECRET SERVICE
AND SUMMARIES OF CONFERENCE RESPONSES


The questions below were originally presented by Robert R. Burke, then Assistant Director of the United States Secret Service, Office of Protective Research, at the November 14, 1980, planning committee meeting held to prepare for this conference.

1.     At what point should a person be considered dangerous?  What are the objective indicators of dangerousness, and what items of information should be collected to make this determination?

Conferees were generally uncomfortable about the labelling of a person as either dangerous or not dangerous.  In their view, dangerousness should not be regarded as a personality trait.  Rather, propensity toward violent or dangerous behavior should be viewed as fluctuating over time and elicited by particular settings, situations, or mental states of the individual.  While some mentally ill persons may be more likely than "normals" to harm others or themselves, this is not the case for most of the mentally disturbed. Clinicians experienced with violent patients can often recognize behavioral indicators of imminent violence and suggest strategies for dealing with such persons, but conferees agreed that no one can make reliable long-term predictions as to whether and when a person might try to harm others or himself.

If a person has behaved in ways agents feel may pose risk to those protected by the Service, he or she must be evaluated or reassessed at frequent intervals to determine present capacity for engaging in violent behavior.  Agents interviewing such a person should find out what has triggered violent behavior in the past and carefully note this information for follow-up purposes.

While many conferees suggested items of information they thought should be included in assessing persons for dangerousness, they admitted that there is as yet no definitive list of factors known to be associated with dangerousness toward protected persons. Much research remains to be done in this area.

2.     Is there an explicit, systematic method of assigning weights and priorities to the various items of information collected for decision-making with respect to assessing dangerousness?

There are techniques available to determine what weights and priorities agents actually use at present to make their dangerousness decisions; there are also methods of specifying how such decisions should be made, given certain assumptions about the relative importance of the various items of information collected. Currently, however, the requisite knowledge base as to which variables are truly associated with dangerousness to protected persons is lacking. Only empirical research in this area will increase understanding of which variables are relevant and to what degree.

3. How can the process of eliciting information from a subject in an interview situation be improved? How should the approach to different types of subjects vary? For instance, when should a stress interview be used or not used?

Conferees had many practical suggestions for improving the yield of information from subjects during an interview; many of these are discussed in presentations and in papers. Conferees offered advice not only about techniques appropriate for interviewing disturbed and potentially dangerous persons, but also about the composition of interview teams, the location of interviews, the frequency of interviewing, interview format, and the times when Secret Service subjects might be interviewed to maximize information yielded. They felt that Secret Service agents could benefit from additional training in interviewing techniques and suggested that the Service test various suggestions in controlled comparisons or "experiments" to see which of them might be worth implementing.

4. What do we know about the potential dangerousness of a person under the influence of a group--particularly an unstable individual?

Conferees participating in one workshop group addressed this question briefly, at the suggestion of the group's Secret Service representative. They tended to agree with Secret Service personnel that the type of person to be most concerned about is the marginal or self-proclaimed member of a fringe group espousing extremist social, political, or religious views, especially a group with a history of violent activity. Such a person is usually not regarded by the group's leadership as a member in good standing, and may use the group to fulfill his or her own personal goals, thereby absolving himself of responsibility for his own actions. Workshop participants did caution the Secret Service not to become distracted by group membership in and of itself, and to be mindful of civil liberties issues in dealing with groups and their members.

5. How can the Secret Service become a more informed consumer of behavioral research?

At present, the Secret Service has extremely limited internal capacity to conduct behavioral research relevant to its mission, or to evaluate such research that may have been done elsewhere. It does, however, employ consultants to assist it in developing research ideas and strategies, to develop and conduct training programs, and to evaluate incoming behavioral research proposals. These consultants can also help the Service become a more informed consumer of behavioral research. Conferees encouraged the Service to continue to use consultants, noting that it would probably always have a need for consultants in particular substantive areas.

As a next step, conferees suggested that an independent research advisory board be created to work with the Secret Service and its consultants in developing behavioral science research priorities, deciding on which of the research suggestions in this conference summary the Service should implement, evaluating incoming research proposals, examining ongoing research in other federal agencies and private institutions in areas relevant to the Secret Service mission, establishing relationships with the scientific and clinical community, and otherwise providing advice and consultation pertinent to the development of a behavioral research capability within the Secret Service itself.

6. Should the Secret Service recruit and organize an internal professional behavioral research staff?

Conferees were in agreement that eventual development of a competent and highly skilled in-house research staff would best serve the needs of the Secret Service. Opinions were divided, however, as to the advisability of attempting to develop such a research capability in the immediate future. Given the small size and relative inexperience of the Secret Service in the area of behavioral research, some conferees doubted that the Service would be able to recruit such talent at this time, and thought the Service would do better by contracting with outsiders to handle most of its research needs. On the other hand, conferees recognized that there must be at least a few "educated consumers" of behavioral research within the Secret Service to be able to communicate research needs and findings to management personnel, evaluate research proposals and funded research, and translate research findings into operationally useful information. The consensus was that the Service should immediately recruit a small, in-house staff to work with its behavioral science consultants and a research advisory board external to the Service, to begin developing its research capability and to implement research recommendations.

7. How can the relationhsip between the Secret Service and the mental health professions be improved?

Conferees agreed that the relationship between the Secret Service and the mental health community should be improved, especially in view of the fact that a very high proportion of the cases presently considered dangerous to protected persons have a history of mental health problems. To develop realistic expectations of each other and an attitude of mutual trust and respect, the Secret Service and the mental health community should, as a first step, become better acquainted with each other's capabilities and limitations, both professionally and institutionally. Whatever the specific nature of the relationships developed, however, conferees were adamant that Secret Service and mental health personnel be at all times aware of their separate and distinct roles and goals when dealing with Secret Service subjects who may be mentally or emotionally disturbed. Similarly, neither Secret Service nor mental health personnel can delegate their own responsibilities to the other. In short, any relationships between the Secret Service and the mental health community should be founded on cooperation without co-optation.

There are two areas in which the mental health community can assist the Secret Service in its task of assessing and managing dangerous persons: (1) it can provide consultation, evaluation, and/or diagnostic assistance with respect to Secret Service cases referred to mental health professionals and institutions, as well as in- or out-patient care, as appropriate, for cases referred; and (2) it can develop training programs for Secret Service special agents in the area of mental disorders. Conferees had many different suggestions for mechanisms by which these two forms of assistance might be provided. Some thought the Secret Service should develop formalized, long-term contractual relationships with particular mental health institutions and professionals to which agents would have access on a regular basis for consultation about cases which present evaluation or management problems. Others thought it preferable for the Secret Service to consult with a variety of mental health institutions and professionals on an informal and ad hoc basis. In the area of training, conferees agreed that Secret Service agents need a greater understanding of psychopathology and its various manifestations, exposure to a wide range of mentally disturbed persons, instruction in interviewing and management techniques appropriate for use with the mentally ill, and greater familiarity with mental health facilities and personnel. Much of the training that agents receive in the area of mental health, they felt, should be hospital-based.

8.   Once a dangerous person is identified, how should he or she be managed, neutralized, deterred within the context of a free society?

Conferees had many suggestions for modifying and enlarging the repertoire of management techniques the Secret Service presently uses to deal with those it considers dangerous to protected persons. They felt that the range of options presently used is too narrow and insufficiently flexible to meet the varied needs and problems presented by different subjects. For instance, in the opinion of many conferees, the Secret Service places too much confidence in the admission of apparently mentally disturbed subjects to hospitals. Typically, this results in a very brief confinement with little or no change in the status of the chronic mental disorder from which the person is suffering. A more appropriate strategy might be to try to arrange for continuing and thorough out-patient psychiatric care.

While almost all intervention strategies run the risk of violating individual civil liberties--especially when no prosecutable offense has been committed--conferees encouraged the Secret Service to explore and use management techniques that are unobstrusive, wherever possible, and in all cases to apply the principle of "least restrictive alternatives" in selecting particular management techniques.

OPENING REMARKS

David A. Hamburg, M.D.*
Director, Division of Health Policy, Research and Education
Harvard University
Cambridge, Massachusetts

This is a distinctive venture, both for the Secret Service and for the Institute of Medicine. It has been my pleasure to work with Director Stuart Knight and his colleagues in undertaking it. At this workshop, we are addressing problems of great national importance.

Who among us can forget those photographs of Dallas almost two decades ago? Those are the most vivid symbols of the awesome responsibility which the Service has and also of the courage and dedication of its staff. As I have gotten to know the leadership of the Service in these past few years, I have been deeply impressed with their professionalism and their resourcefulness. Stuart Knight has brought open-minded, farsighted leadership. The Service is open to new ideas and not defensive.

We must face the fact of assassination as a part of the warp and woof of our culture and of many others. We have all preferred in this society to believe that these events are somehow rare, peculiar, haphazard and unlikely to occur again, at least for a long time; but the evidence is really overwhelming that assassination is a clear, present, and continuing danger to our political leaders. It is painful to face the reality of the frequently recurrent nature of such behavior and to recognize the powerful ramifications of leadership assassination. It seems to me that these ramifications have been profoundly damaging in our lifetime in this country; and they have adversely affected the way this country is viewed by the rest of the world. Surely there is no basis for complacency. If anything, we have more reason to be more concerned than we might have had two decades ago.

There are many factors that give me concern: the instant availability of lethal weapons, the mobility of potential assassins, the media-facilitated contagion of hatred and of formulas for

---

*President, Institute of Medicine, National Academy of Sciences, 1975-1980.

13

assassination or other terrorist behavior, the upsurge of fanaticism both in this country and abroad, the spread of terrorism in many forms, and the vulnerability of our political leaders. The repeated killing or serious wounding of our leaders can have deeply pathological effects on democratic society.

In a democratic society, who really does select our leaders? Do the voters? Does the free interplay of ideas and open competition of values? Or do assassins select our leaders?

What can the Secret Service do with its awesome responsibility that it is not doing now? Is there anything more that the Service could possibly do that would make sense? The Service is here engaged in a constructive, restless searching--pushing at the boundaries of knowledge and skill. We should join them in this quest. We should help them to utilize the best available information from the scientific community about dangerous behavior and different ways of dealing with it.

In principle, there should be value in a periodic update, in a regular flow of information and ideas bearing on the problems faced by the Service. These are long-term problems. There is an enduring set of issues with which they and we have to cope. Moreover, there is the real possibility of stimulating some additional research as suggested, for example, in the paper that Lincoln Moses* submitted for this workshop.

I think it is, also, a part of our responsibility to help the Secret Service to face limitations in knowledge at any given time and to seek alternative strategies of protection in light of limitations of knowledge. The problems of this workshop have been of interest and concern to us for many years. As I have become increasingly familiar with the dilemmas involved, I have concluded that the most likely way of making a major gain in protecting leaders would be through changes in their own behavior. The stakes are exceedingly high, and we must not assume that our political life is too rigid to permit adequate protection for our highest elected officials. Any prudent leader should know that there is a very high risk. It is only sensible to assume that any president or major presidential candidate is at high risk of assassination.

There may have been brief intervals when presidents and even presidential candidates have met what we might properly call a presidential standard of behavior--i.e., behavior that is cautious and prudent in light of the knowledge of the high risks to which such

---

*"Learning from Experience, the Secret Service, and Controlled Experimentation," included in this conference summary, page 113.

people are exposed. The issue for national leaders is not to prove their courage by exposing themselves to assassins; their calling is a higher one.

In toxicology, one thinks about risk as a function both of toxicity and exposure. In this case, toxicity is very high. Therefore, the issue centers on ways in which exposure can be minimized. We must consider a wide range of options for diminishing exposure below our present dangerous levels.

There is another task that we are not asked to address at the moment but that will become salient at some future time. The Service does all in its power to keep its staff in good health, high morale, and strong professionalism; but theirs is a highly stressful occupation. When the Institute of Medicine's current study on stress and disease is completed, its insights might well be applied to the Service in efforts directed toward the maintenance of health.

The Institute of Medicine is a good focal point for interplay between the Service and the scientific community over a wide range of behavior as well as other sciences pertinent to health. So, in addition to the intrinsic value of this occasion, it may set in motion some long-term relationship of value to American society. We are dealing here with a set of functions in a democratic society that are crucial to the effective functioning of the electorate and the maintenance of core democratic values.

OPENING REMARKS

H. S. Knight
Director
United States Secret Service
Washington, D. C.


It was perhaps a year or so ago when we first explored with Dr. Hamburg the possibilities of convening a workshop such as this, with the expectation that you might give us some help. That is the key word: help. It is not the cry of a drowning man. I don't want to mislead you. We think we are doing reasonably well in what we are now doing--some of you might say we have delusions of adequacy--but in an organization dedicated to excellence, "reasonably well" just does not quite make it. We want to improve on that.

We want to ask you to explore with us the definition of the goals that we think we have, refine the techniques that we now employ, examine what tools we are now using and whether we are using them in a proper way and what tools we might not have that you think would be beneficial to us.

We are asking you to tell us whether we are doing the right thing in the right way. This can and will be a good exercise in theory, but what we are hoping for--what we are looking for--are some data, some practical hints and suggestions that we can utilize in our day-to-day activities. I don't overstate it when I say that every agent faces a "day-to-day confrontation" with this problem on the street. We hope that out of this will come something that we can pass on to our special agents that will help them do their job better. I think if you can help us, you will, in a broader sense, be helping society.

We recognize that there is no magic solution. To oversimplify, what we are asking you to do is to help refine our task of trying to predict individual human behavior. And I do wish you success. I am impressed with the assemblage, and I hope that all of our people will be as helpful to you as they possibly can be, because it is only with that kind of an attitude that we can jointly come up with something that will be beneficial to all.

SECRET SERVICE EXPECTATIONS FROM THE CONFERENCE

Robert A. Snow
Acting Assistant Director
Office of Protective Research
United States Secret Service
Washington, D. C.


When I was a young agent in Buffalo, New York, I was sent to Washington on a temporary assignment to work the Inauguration activities for President Kennedy, and then I was held over for the State of the Union speech.

I will always remember my post at that State of the Union speech. It was in the balcony of the House, right up next to the clock, right over the Speaker's stand. During the speech, I found myself looking out over the group and seeing our Joint Chiefs of Staff in their full uniforms and the Justices of the Supreme Court in their black robes and the new cabinet the President had recently appointed; and here was the President, the Vice President, the Speaker of the House, and that was my entire government sitting there out in front of me, and I will always remember that feeling of awe that I had, standing there looking at that and having that experience.

I have somewhat the same feeling today. I look out over this group and see the current positions you hold, the various credentials you bring to this meeting, the contributions you have made to your disciplines; and I have that same feeling of awe and I guess expectation as to what can be accomplished for the Secret Service in the next two days.

Last November when we addressed the members of the planning committee for the workshop, my predecessor, Assistant Director Bob Burke, presented a list of questions and issues for consideration and study. I understand most of you had the chance to review these before coming. In the interest of brevity, because there is a great deal of work to do in the next couple of days, I would just like to co-opt those questions by way of reference.

I would emphasize that the list is not, of course, cast in stone. It should not be considered all-inclusive or all-embracing. The questions are intended merely as starters for your thinking. We recognize they are not couched in scientific language, but I think we

19

are going to leave that up to you, the experts, to turn them around and see what we are talking about. I have one further point about the questions. Collectively, they represent strictly our perceptions of the problems. We hope you will see them as that and interject your own, because many of the thoughts and ideas that have already come out have been extremely valuable.

Director Knight and Special Agent-in-Charge of the Intelligence Division Ed Walsh talked about the problems in predicting human behavior, and the attendant conceptualizations, interpretations, assumptions, and self-imposed constraints. We all know it is not infrequent that very complex problems are perceived initially as insoluble, but often with just a turn of mind or a fresh perception or a new way of asking a question, we can shed considerable light on those apparently insoluble problems. I am confident that you can read between the lines and see the challenge here. We have had these perceptions, and we have been asking the same questions for a number of years without getting very far. This is why we are now reaching out to you for this kind of creative thinking.

I would say, though, without trying to constrain your creative thinking ability, that we must stress in the final analysis that your ideas, suggestions and recommendations must meet the test of practicality. The realities of time constraints, limited resources, and human nature permeate our daily routines.

During the last couple of months you have all met with Bob Kyanko and Dwight Colley--one or the other, sometimes both--and with a field office representative. I hope that you found these brief exchanges useful and informative. I know from their standpoint it was extremely beneficial.

During the last few days, I have had the opportunity to read several papers and memoranda that some of you have prepared and submitted. I and other staff people are delighted with the quality and resourcefulness of the thinking evident in just these few papers.

I have a strong sense of confidence that the next two days will be very important in the history of the Secret Service. You should be aware that as participants in this endeavor you are part of an historical event. This cooperative endeavor, its nature and magnitude, are unprecedented in our 115 year history. This is a true milestone. It is something brand new to us, and we are truly looking forward to what can come of it.

I would like to leave you with one final thought--a couple of lines from the sonnets of Edna St. Vincent Millay. I believe the words capture the rationale and the thrust of this entire conference:

. . . . . . . . . . . . . . . . . . . . . . .
Upon this gifted age, in its dark hour,
Rains from the sky a meteoric shower
Of facts . . . they lie unquestioned, uncombined.
Wisdom enough to leach us of our ill
Is daily spun; but there exists no loom
To weave it into fabric . . . .*

Now maybe we can start building that loom.

*Edna St. Vincent Millay, from "Huntsman, What Quarry?,"
Collected Poems (New York:  Harper and Row, 1956).

SUMMARY OF WORKSHOP AND PLENARY DISCUSSIONS

Each conference participant, including Institute of Medicine staff and Secret Service representatives and consultants, attended one of three workshops held on both days of the conference. Workshop sessions were conducted simultaneously and discussions ranged across the entire subject matter of the conference. Workshops were chaired by Elissa P. Benedek and Robert Michels (Group A), Shervert H. Frazier (Group B), and Charles H. Whitebread (Group C).

Workshop discussions, together with discussion preceding and following presentations during plenary sessions, are summarized under the following major headings:

# Introduction

This conference of behavioral scientists and clinicians was convened to bring their knowledge to bear on the problems of identifying, assessing, and monitoring persons likely to threaten the safety of those the Secret Service protects. The conferees hoped to assist the Secret Service Intelligence Division in devising responsible and appropriate ways to determine the effectiveness of its information-gathering activities and interventions with persons and groups of concern.[1]

The Secret Service Intelligence Division is daily faced with a great many difficult decisions--about the likely dangerousness of each case brought to its attention, about the management of those believed to pose risk to persons protected by the Service, and as to whether persons formerly considered dangerous are still a source of risk, to name a few. These decisions must be made under conditions of considerable uncertainty and high risk. Predicting human behavior with any degree of accuracy is difficult at best, and errors in judgment can have consequences as grave as the assassination of the president of the United States.

## ASSESSING POTENTIALLY DANGEROUS BEHAVIOR

About 20 new cases per day are brought to the attention of the Intelligence Division. These cases are referred to Secret Service field offices throughout the country, where they are assigned to special agents for investigation. For each new case, or "subject" in Secret Service terminology, special agents must make a dangerousness determination within five to 14 days, depending on the priority of the case: they must decide whether the subject is to be classified as "dangerous" or "not dangerous" to persons protected by the Service.

In the course of making their dangerousness determinations, Secret Service special agents are required to collect a great deal of information about the subject: demographic and identification data (address, place of work, date of birth, marital status, aliases used, and so forth); information about the subject's education, training, and skills, including familiarity with weapons; family history; mental history; criminal history; citizenship status; military service record; addictions and deviations; organizational affiliations; and "directions of interest" (those persons or targets about whom the subject has expressed or otherwise indicated hostile or unusual interest). Handwriting samples, photographs, and other identification materials are also collected if deemed relevant. The dangerousness decision is usually made before the investigation of the subject has been completed. Once all relevant information has been assembled, agents file a written report, which contains the findings of the investigation, the dangerousness determination, all correspondence from and about the subject, and any other pertinent materials. Portions of this report are stored in a computer at Secret Service headquarters.

To obtain information about a subject, special agents typically interview him or her in person and consult a variety of other sources and records, including the FBI, military or hospital records, and the subject's family, friends, or associates. For subjects they consider dangerous, special agents must devise ways to keep track of their activities, manage their behavior, or otherwise reduce the risk they pose to protected persons.*

The vast majority of all subjects investigated by special agents are judged not dangerous. Approximately 300 subjects out of a total of some 26,000 fully investigated subjects on file with the Secret Service are presently considered dangerous. (The remainder have never been considered dangerous or were considered dangerous at some time in the past.)

### Problems of Making Determinations about Dangerousness

The dangerousness determinations that must be made by special agents involve estimates or "predictions" about future behaviors, and are always made under conditions of uncertainty and high risk. Although agents try to reduce uncertainty by obtaining as much information about the subject as possible before they make their decisions, Secret Service personnel are not sure that the information routinely collected is directly relevant to predicting whether a subject will or will not engage in behavior that might actually harm a protected person. They have also expressed concern about how the various items of information collected should be best used to make a decision.** At present, special agents base their dangerousness decisions on their admittedly subjective impressions gained during interviews with subjects and on a few specific items of information, which may differ from agent to agent. The Secret Service hoped that conferees would have some suggestions for improving agent decision-making processes, making them more reliable and valid.

---

*Interventions and management techniques used with subjects considered dangerous are discussed under Management of Dangerous Subjects, page 59.

**See Questions Raised by the Secret Service and Summaries of Conference Responses, page 7.

Conferees emphasized that prediction, judgment, and making decisions are highly fallible and difficult tasks, even under the best of circumstances, and that Secret Service personnel should not expect a panel of experts to be able to help them improve their capability in these areas to a dramatic degree. Thus, the Service should expect modest and incremental gains, and not "breakthroughs" as a result of conferee suggestions in these areas.

Several reasons underlay this less than optimistic viewpoint. First, accurate prediction of individual behavior has been demonstrated repeatedly to be largely unsuccessful, even when a great deal is known about the persons whose behavior is being predicted and predicted behaviors themselves, and when those making the predictions are experts in the relevant fields.* Conferees unanimously agreed that behavior likely to occur in the distant future is predicted with much less success than behavior expected to occur in the very near future. In fact, the shorter the time span between the prediction and the expected behavior, the more likely the prediction will be accurate. Thus, any attempt to predict that a Secret Service subject is or is not likely to be dangerous to a protected person is apt to be useless unless a very limited time frame is considered. Second, when the behavior being predicted occurs infrequently--or has a "low base rate"--accurate prediction of who will and will not engage in it is even less likely. Assassination and assassination attempts on political leaders are rare events, at least in the United States,** particularly with respect to persons presently protected by the Secret Service. Under such circumstances, the behavior is bound to be overpredicted. That is, there will be many "false positives" among those predicted to engage in the behavior--persons identified as potential assassins who will not attempt to assassinate a

---

*See presentation by John Monahan, page 129.

**An impression that U. S. history is rife with presidential assassination attempts may be caused by their high proportion--10 of 40 presidents have been attacked--but the attackers total only 12, including the man alleged to have shot President Reagan March 30, 1981. (President Ford was the subject of two separate assassination attempts, and President Truman was the subject one attempt involving two assailants.).

protected person.* A third problem is that human judgment and decision-making are known to be highly fallible and inconsistent, even among so-called experts.** Yet another problem compounds the difficulties of making accurate predictions of subject behavior: because the Secret Service cannot take the risk of not intervening with a subject when it thinks it should, the Service is to some extent unable to learn whether its predictions as to dangerousness are successful or not. The possibility, however slim, that an untoward event might occur makes non-intervention unacceptable in view of the Service's mandate to "protect," with the result that the Service is limited in its capacity to evaluate the level of effectiveness of its own operations.

Acknowledging the fallibility of human judgment, many conferees nevertheless agreed with Kenneth Hammond that development of a "decision support system" might assist special agents in their judgments about dangerousness and other matters. A decision support system is a method by which the advice and skills of specialists can be made available through computer modelling. Specialists in various fields considered relevant to the decision, such as psychiatry, psychology, and criminal justice, can provide support by identifying the variables which they themselves consider important in assessing persons for dangerousness, and make their own decision processes available for scrutiny and computer modelling. Additionally, a cadre of such experts could be on call to assist agents personally in deciding how to evaluate difficult cases.

The Concept of Dangerousness

While it may be necessary from an administrative standpoint to have special agents decide that a subject is dangerous or not dangerous, many conferees questioned the appropriateness and

---

*Some suggestions for dealing with the problem of low-base-rate behaviors are discussed under Suggested Approaches to the Study of Assassination, page 44, and in memoranda by Monahan and Franklin Zimring, pages 179 and 183, respectively.

**See memorandum by Kenneth Hammond, page 175.

relevance of this dichotomy for subsequent decisions about subjects.*  A simple division of all subjects into categories dangerous and not dangerous fails to recognize that (1) dangerousness is not an enduring personality trait, but rather a state that may be dependent on many factors; (2) the extent to which a subject may pose risk to a protected person will vary over time and with circumstances; and (3) persons vary considerably in the level of risk they may pose, and cannot be considered simply dangerous or not dangerous.  Some conferees, including psychiatrists Robert Michels and Loren Roth, questioned the utility of making dangerousness determinations at all, because such decisions at any one time are likely to be highly unreliable and invalid.**  The important and relevant task for Secret Service agents, as for clinical psychiatrists, they said, is to devise a management plan or, in Michels' words, "a process for making an infinite series of decisions" about how the subject should be handled to neutralize or otherwise mitigate the hostility he or she manifests toward protected persons.

Many conferees felt that if the concept of dangerousness is to be retained and used for decision-making about subjects, the Secret Service should explore and attempt to develop indicators that would permit subjects to be rated and compared with each other in terms of the relative risk they pose to protected persons and also in terms of their own level of dangerousness at different points in time.  In the category of dangerous subjects, the Service should be more explicit about the level of concern it has about each subject in relation to all others and about each subject over time, and should develop behavioral indicators to measure these gradations in dangerousness.  Such an exercise and its application would help the Service begin to identify not only whom it should be most concerned about and when, but also what behaviors might be immediate preludes to assassination attempts.

## Mental Illness and Dangerousness

Approximately 90 percent of all persons the Secret Service presently considers dangerous to protected persons gave some indication of mental disorder before coming to the attention of the Service.  Conferees were particularly interested in determining why this is so, and whether the level of concern with the mentally ill is

---

*Secret Service representatives noted that if a third category were added, falling between the two extremes, agents would be tempted to overuse it.

**See Roth's memorandum, page 181.

justified. They also offered a variety of suggestions for assessing and managing emotionally disturbed subjects.

Secret Service concern with emotionally disturbed people who make threats against protected persons may to some extent reflect the widespread popular belief that the mentally ill are violence-prone. Because of their relative unfamiliarity with mental illness, Secret Service special agents may tend to view the behavior of the mentally ill as dangerous because it seems so unpredictable, while the behaviors of those without apparent mental disorder may seem more rational. (No data were available on the incidence of mental disorder among subjects the Secret Service has never considered dangerous.)

Conferees emphasized that much violent behavior is state-dependent, occurring only at times when the person in question is in specific situations, under particular stresses, or in a particular state of mind. For example, a person may pose risk while intoxicated, but not at other times. A manic patient may be violent only when off medication. As pointed out by Roth, a competent clinical examination of a patient or subject known or anticipated to be violent should always involve a "meticulous examination of the past violent episodes or . . . threats in terms of what state the person was in."*

### Role of Mental Health Professionals in Assessing Dangerousness

Many clinicians felt that mental health professionals have relatively little to offer in the way of predicting whether and when a Secret Service subject might attempt to harm a protected person. In their opinion, Secret Service agents are probably as expert in this area as anyone, and perhaps more so than many mental health professionals, given agents' extensive experience in responding to "threats" and other behavioral manifestations of hostile intent toward protected persons. Although certain clinicians experienced with violent patients may be fairly well equipped to predict imminent violence, mental health professionals in general have not been shown to be better than anyone else in making predictions about behavior which might occur in the distant future under changing conditions. Clinicians and others felt particularly uncomfortable about the notion of classifying subjects as either dangerous or not dangerous, for reasons discussed earlier. The probability that a Secret Service subject will do violence to others or himself is likely to fluctuate

---

*This topic is also addressed by Shervert Frazier in his presentation, page 133, and by R. Kirkland Gable in his memorandum, page 171.

over time and must be reevaluated through periodic (or nearly continuous) monitoring. Thus, clinicians preferred to view the task of assessment for dangerousness as an ongoing process and not distinct from the monitoring and management tasks to which special agents are also assigned.

For the purpose of assessing subjects for dangerousness, conferees agreed that mental health professionals might usefully provide Secret Service agents with

● greater understanding of the course and fluctuations of mental disorders and emotional disturbances over time, and the relationship between diagnostic categories and behavior

● assistance in identifying subpopulations of the mentally ill who are or might be dangerous to others or themselves

● guidance concerning the types of questions or items to include in interview protocols to assess risk

● techniques for interviewing potentially dangerous persons*

● ad hoc consultation in the evaluation (assessment) of difficult, puzzling, or ambiguous cases.

## Effect of Group Affinity on an Unstable Person

In assessing a subject for dangerousness, Secret Service special agents routinely inquire about the subject's group affiliations. Although the Service has no concrete evidence about the influence of groups on individual behavior, agents do tend to have a higher level of concern about a subject who belongs to or identifies with a radical extremist group, particularly if the group espouses unusual religious or political beliefs and has a history of violent activity.

In its desire to know more about the influence of groups on individual behavior, the Service asked conferees to consider the question, "What do we know about the potential dangerousness of a person under the influence of a group--particularly an unstable individual?". Although this topic did not constitute a separate agenda item at the conference, one workshop group explored it briefly, at the request of its Secret Service representative.

---

*See Frazier's presentation and paper by Frazier and colleagues, pages 133 and 93, respectively.

Secret Service consultant Edwin Megargee said that there is a large body of theory and empirical research on the psychology of groups and group behavior, and on the functions of group membership for the individual.  In general, an unstable person may be motivated to join a group out of a desire to enhance his status by association with its influential members, or to be able to diffuse or suspend a sense of personal responsibility for his actions.  Such persons may be inclined to engage in activities they think will please the group leadership.  Conferees noted that the leadership of groups with a serious mission (however farfetched or irrational that mission may seem to outsiders) are perennially concerned about the marginal individual who fancies himself to be a member in good standing and is eager to serve, but who is likely to blunder while attempting to fulfill his own personal needs in the name of the group.

Conferees tended to agree with the Secret Service in its concern about unstable persons who identify with radical groups.  Brian Jenkins said he would be most worried about fringe members of fringe groups.

Workshop discussants did not directly address the issue of the potential dangerousness of the leadership of such groups, though one conferee cautioned that group leaders can be extremely manipulative and attempt to engage a police organization such as the Secret Service in "guerilla warfare" to achieve their goals.  Such skirmishes can be extremely unpleasant as well as exhausting for a government agency, and may even escalate to violence.  Charles Whitebread was of the opinion that police organizations tend to become unduly distracted by groups--particularly those they do not like--and by the very fact that an individual belongs to a (radical) group.  He advised the Service to be mindful of civil liberties issues when dealing with such groups and their members.

### Assessment Procedures:  Suggestions for Improvement

On the basis of what they learned in pre-conference briefings and in plenary and workshop sessions, conferees made a number of suggestions for improving the information collected about subjects, the field procedures and instruments used, the written reports detailing the findings of subject investigations, and information storage and retrieval procedures.

### Information Collected

Conferees questioned the relevance of some of the specific items of information the Secret Service presently collects.  For instance, some wondered whether sexual preference (homosexuality or heterosexuality) bears any relationship to whether a person might or might not be harmful to protected persons. They also noted that, typically, much of the information collected is not used in making dangerousness decisions or is collected after decisions are made to be on record should the need arise. That is, the relationship between the data collected and the outcome being predicted by the agents' decisions (i.e., dangerous or not dangerous) is unclear. As previously noted, Secret Service representatives readily acknowledge that present decisions result from a largely subjective process, not systematically or consistently related to the data collected from subjects and other sources.

Inventory of Potentially Relevant Assessment Items    Conferees reached no conclusions as to which items of information are relevant for decisions about dangerousness, but they did suggest that the Secret Service devote serious attention to this issue and perhaps engage some outside help in revising its present list of items investigated by special agents.*

Because relatively little is presently known about the items of information that are truly related to dangerousness, conferees suggested that the Service anticipate that whatever items are included in the revised data collection list will have to be further refined over time, with those items empirically determined to be irrelevant eliminated and perhaps replaced by new ones. The goal should be to reduce the amount of data collected to only a few items, which are shown by experience and research to be highly predictive with respect to dangerousness to protected persons. This goal, however, will not be achieved without extensive trial and error, and should not be regarded as attainable in the near future.

Conferees said that data collected and recorded about subjects should be directly relevant to decision tasks, and not merely for record keeping purposes.

Conferees also felt that the notion of relative risk should be built into the data collection system. That is, response categories to questions asked of subjects and others interviewed in the process of investigation should enable agents to rank order subjects in terms of their level of dangerousness with respect to each other and also with respect to themselves at different points in time. (This issue will be discussed further below.)

---

*One list of data elements suggested for use in the assessment process was proposed by Frazier and colleagues in their paper.

At the outset of an investigation, conferees suggested, the Secret Service should be collecting information about the motivations, feelings, and attitudes of subjects toward protected persons; current psychological functioning and mental history; criminal history; weapons knowledge and weapons procurement activities; subject mobility and other indicators of ability to carry out threats or inflict harm on protected persons; and a variety of factual background data. (The Secret Service already collects information about most of these items, as indicated earlier.)

The members of one workshop group compiled a list of factors they felt should give cause for concern, if evidenced by subjects during interviews or if otherwise ascertained. They also noted a few factors they thought might indicate decreased risk to protected persons. They did not, however, specify the relative importance of any of these factors in assessing risk to protected persons, nor did they suggest how these factors might be used collectively to reach dangerousness decisions.

The following were suggested as possible indicators of increased risk: history of emergency psychiatric admission(s), history of extremely bizarre behavior, claims of personal relationships with protected persons that are remote, lack of concern for self-preservation, concern on the part of significant others about the subject's behavior; fixed ideas, obsessions, or compulsions concerning one or more protected persons; extreme or seemingly irrational hostility toward protected persons; evidence of intense interest in a protected person as suggested by such things as the presence of their travel routes or itineraries in the subject's home; repeated or frequent threats to harm a protected person; episodic or binge drinking, history of alcoholic blackouts; involvement in fringe organizations with a history of violence; history of unemployment or employment difficulties; presence of situational stresses (such as recent losses or life changes) that might interact with underlying mental disorder; absence of social supports (family, friends); "wanderlust" (no permanent home or participation in stable social relationships); exaggerated concern with the world situation; idiosyncratic gripes against the government, and especially feelings of having been cheated or taken advantage of by the government; presence of hate literature in the home; caches of weapons in the home; indicators of ability to follow through on or carry out threats; and evidence of past killing.*

---

*There was disagreement as to the relevance of this factor. Some conferees thought it important to determine the context in which the killing had occurred and felt that having killed legitimately (as in time of war) would not be a relevant factor. Others thought that the fact of having killed another human being, whatever the context, was relevant.

In someone already being followed up by the Secret Service, any of the following changes in status, coupled with the protected person traveling to the subject's area of residence, could indicate increased risk:  increases in drug or alcohol use, loss of job, or loss of a significant stabilizing relationship.

The following factors were viewed as indicators of decreased risk:  stable employment, a stable family situation and other conventional bonds, the presence of children, extreme psychological disorganization, and low intelligence.

Field Procedures and Instruments Used

Conferees were unanimously agreed that the personal interview is an indispensable tool for assessing the potential dangerousness of subjects, even though it may be an inherently stressful experience for many special agents.  A personal interview can yield not only hard information about a subject (which may be valuable for subsequent identification and management purposes), but also can provide many clues to the motivations and dynamics of a subject's interest in protected persons.  Most special agents assessing subjects for dangerousness find the personal interview to be the most helpful source of information for decision-making.

A few conferees, aware of the fact that most special agents assigned to the task of assessing subjects for dangerousness are white middle class males, suggested that male-female teams of interviewers might be more successful than male-only interview teams in eliciting a full range of useful information from subjects.  (This suggestion could be experimented with on a limited basis to test its validity.)  They also felt that female interviewers, whether or not they are teamed with male interviewers, should be used when interviewing female subjects.*

Noting that some threat activity and other behaviors considered potentially dangerous to protected persons are "state dependent," other conferees, notably R. Kirkland Gable and Loren Roth, suggested that interviewing and assessing subjects during periods when they engage in these behaviors might be useful.  For an alcholic who threatens only when drunk, for example, more relevant information about his intentions might be forthcoming when he is intoxicated than when he is sober.  Similarly, for a manic depressive subject who appears to pose risk when in a manic state, interviewing him or her

_____

*See presentation by Frazier and paper by Frazier and colleagues, pages 133 and 93, respectively.

during a manic episode might be illuminating. This may involve interviewing such persons while they are hospitalized.

Special agents are instructed to elicit information on the list of topics mentioned earlier, but there is no standard and prescribed format for conducting the interview or reporting the information from it in written form. Interviews are open-ended: all topics are covered, but the order in which questions are asked is not specified, nor must questions be worded in a particular way. Rather, agents pursue leads and ask follow-up questions as the interview situation seems to dictate. Some conferees suggested that the data collection effort would be both more reliable and more useful for decision-making (and subsequent research and analysis) if a standard format and structured interview protocol were used. Others felt, however, that if a more structured format is adopted, the use of imaginative probes and follow-up questions based on hunches and intuitions should also be permitted and encouraged.

Information about subjects is elicited not only from the subjects themselves, but from a variety of sources, making it likely that there will be factual discrepancies among sources. For instance, agents may hear one set of facts about his employment history from the subject himself and a different set from his spouse or close associate. Some clinicians wondered how such discrepancies are recorded and resolved.

Scaling Dangerous Attitudes and Behaviors   As indicated earlier, conferees urged the Secret Service to build the notion of relative risk into its data collection instruments. They felt that too much emphasis is placed on determining whether a subject is or is not dangerous and not enough attention devoted to rank ordering the level of risk the subject poses in relation to other subjects at a particular time, and in relation to the attitudes and behaviors the subject might exhibit at some future date. One method of building gradations in dangerousness into the assessment procedure is to scale the response categories to questions involving attitudes and behaviors thought to be related to dangerousness. In the virtual absence of the criterion behaviors (assassination and attempted assassination) among subjects, conferees suggested that an index of undesirable events or threshold behaviors short of assassination be developed. One such behavior might be writing a letter in which the subject expresses a desire to blow up the White House. While this behavior might indicate that the subject is dangerous to the president and members of his family, it would be considered less dangerous than evidence that the subject is tracking the president by plotting his itinerary on maps at home, which in turn would be less dangerous than evidence that the subject appeared in proximity to the president with a weapon or stalked him with a weapon on several occasions. Attitudes could similarly be scaled to indicate the level of danger posed by the subject in relation to other subjects at a particular point in time, and in relation to attitudes manifested by the subject when reassessed in the future.

## Written Reports and Information Storage and Retrieval

As noted earlier, dangerousness decisions are frequently made independent of the (sometimes vast amount of) information collected and reported on a subject. Written reports typically contain a great deal of narrative material from which it is difficult to cull relevant information. Although information about a subject in narrative form may be useful for some purposes (such as for advance work when a protected person travels to a subject's area of residence), narrative portions should be written in such a way that the information relevant to decision-making is readily apparent; alternatively or additionally, information should be extracted from the narrative material, coded, and stored in the computer for retrieval and analysis. In short, the written reporting requirements should be carefully examined, and unnecessary narrative material eliminated.

## Consensus Suggestions for Improving the Assessment Process

Conferees reached substantial agreement that the following suggestions would considerably improve the task of assessing Secret Service subjects for dangerousness:

● The entire assessment process should be standardized and rationalized. The information collected, field procedures and instruments used, and the reporting and information storage and retrieval process should be streamlined and made uniform across all cases.

● Data collected and filed on each subject should be directly relevant to decision-making. Careful attention should be directed to determining which items of information are pertinent to decision-making, and these should be retained or eliminated according to their empirically demonstrated utility.

● A more efficient information storage and retrieval system should be developed. Questionnaire items used to collect data on subjects should be precoded for computer use, and all relevant data should be stored in the computer in an easily manipulable form and readily available for use.

● Data collection instruments should contain many scaled items that facilitate rank ordering of behaviors and attitudes of subjects in terms of the degree of danger different subjects pose to protected persons.

● The written report form should be redesigned to highlight relevant information.

● A decision support system would be a useful device to assist agents in making their dangerousness decisions.


## IDENTIFYING POSSIBLE SOURCES OF DANGER TO PROTECTED PERSONS


One of the critical concerns of the Secret Service Intelligence Division is to learn whether it is currently identifying and monitoring those persons most likely to pose risk to the safety of those it protects. Of the roughly 26,000 cases that the Service has investigated, approximately 300 subjects are presently considered dangerous to one or more persons protected by the Secret Service. The number of dangerous cases varies from day to day, as new cases are added and others (no longer considered dangerous) are dropped.


### Current Case Referral and Case Finding Procedures

The majority of cases the Secret Service investigates are referred by the White House, law enforcement agencies, and other federal, state, and local government agencies. Foreign intelligence, private organizations, and individual citizens are other sources of referrals. To identify organized or terrorist threats to protected persons, the Service uses a network of interagency and international contacts developed for this purpose.

Typically, cases referred to the Secret Service for investigation involve threats, either orally or in writing, to harm one or more protected persons, or other indications of risk to such persons, if unchecked. In accordance with Secret Service guidelines, for instance, the White House mail room forwards letters containing references to assassination or terrorist activity, direct or implied threats toward anyone, extremely abusive or obscene language, and mention of unusual grievances against the government or exaggerated demands of protected persons, among other things. White House telephone operators refer phone calls meeting essentially the same criteria. White House visitors, or "callers," whose language or activities appear to pose risk to protected persons are referred to the Service's Washington field office.

## Observations and Suggestions for Improvement

Many conferees questioned the adequacy and comprehensiveness of current referral and case finding practices. First, they had serious reservations as to whether present procedures would necessarily alert the Service to all potential sources of danger to protected persons. They were also concerned about possible misunderstandings and communication failures, even on the part of government entities with well established referral procedures.

Some conferees noted that, apart from receiving some information on the activities of groups, almost all incoming referrals are from announced or self-identified threateners—persons who, through their oral or written communications or other behaviors have already revealed their hostility or sinister intentions and desires. Several conferees pointed out that some persons who do not signify their feelings and intentions beforehand may, in fact, be far more lethal than announced threateners. Some threateners may simply be engaging in expressive behavior and have no serious intention of inflicting harm on protected persons. The same might apply to many of those who repeatedly threaten to harm protected persons. The Secret Service, of course, is well aware of this possibility.*

Upon investigation by Secret Service special agents, many announced threateners are found to have a history of mental or emotional disorders. Clinicians and other conferees pointed out, however, that while some mentally ill or emotionally disturbed persons may be violent under some circumstances, many will never be violent; and they cautioned that the Service's concern with disturbed persons may be unwarranted in many cases and deflect attention and resources from more viable sources of danger. Further, as noted by some conferees, including Loren Roth, in most instances considerable cognitive ability, capacity to plan, and personal organization would be required to penetrate the Secret Service defensive system and actually carry out an assassination. Highly "disorganized" persons would most probably be unable to muster the personal resources to carry out a threat, no matter how ominous their communications may seem. While some of the mentally ill may give "signals" (however unclear to the layman) that they are on the brink of attempting an assassination, in Walter Menninger's words, "I don't expect that real assassins are going to provide the prior clues . . . [Secret Service agents typically] get from the mentally ill threateners." Michels suggested that persons in need of psychiatric care but who have never sought it and have not been evaluated by mental health professionals

---

*See presentation by Brian Jenkins, page 145, on the credibility of threat messages.

might pose greater risk than the mentally disturbed who have been evaluated and treated. The Secret Service is, of course, not unaware of these points.

As Saleem Shah summed up the gist of this argument, a person "not foolish enough to open his mouth," and not obviously mentally ill might be able to evade the intelligence network and penetrate the Secret Service security system.

Not all conferees shared this view, however. Marvin Wolfgang, for instance, noted that among successful assassins there might also be those who give no thought to escape and are willing to die in the process of assassinating their target. For such cases, he said, "one does not need a high degree of planning" nor "a high degree of intelligence."*

Elissa Benedek and others noted the possibility--indeed probability--that the present referral system might be less than fully dependable. This may be so, despite the fact that, in the view of Secret Service representatives, there has been renewed spirit of interagency cooperation in recent years, and it is in the best interests of the referring agency to notify the Secret Service routinely and promptly when a case appears to pose "protective intelligence" problems. Flaws in the referral process might be the result of administrative inefficiencies on the part of the referring agency, or insufficient understanding or genuine differences of opinion as to what, whom, and when to refer.**

Non-Traditional Sources of Risk to Protected Persons

In the opinion of some conferees, the Secret Service at present may be too preoccupied with the mentally disturbed and with persons who fit the profile of a would-be assassin found in the report of the National Commission on the Causes and Prevention of Violence: a white male "loner," often with a history of maladjustment and marginality, likely to be acting on his own rather than as a part of

---

*Secret Service personnel are particularly concerned about subjects who evidence suicidal tendencies, especially when combined with extreme hostility with or without overt threats toward one or more protected persons. The Service monitors such subjects very closely, in the awareness that they are unlikely to be deterred by conventional sanctions.


**The Secret Service does issue referral guidelines to law enforcement and other government agencies.

a conspiracy.*  More attention, they felt, should be devoted to anticipating new and different potential sources of danger:  women and minorities, terrorists, violent radical extremists, and political dissidents or persons and groups with legitimate policy concerns or grievances against the government (in contrast to persons whose political concerns are driven by mental illness), to name a few. More time devoted to case finding among such types of persons and groups might be well spent, they felt, in view of rapid changes in the social, economic, and political climate in the United States and abroad in recent years, which make past experiences with assassination and assassins less appropriate as guides for the future.

As pointed out by Secret Service representatives, however, identifying and monitoring potential but as yet "unannounced" threats to the safety of protected political leaders could be extremely difficult from a technical standpoint; and, as Loren Roth noted, could infringe on the civil rights of persons so identified.


Women and Minorities

A number of conferees, including Elissa Benedek, Sara Eddy, and Robert Fein, advised the Secret Service to take the possibility of women as assassins very seriously.  Menninger noted that the previous two attempted presidential assassins were females.**  And Secret Service representatives mentioned they thought the number of women making threats against protected persons was on the rise (though they had no precise figures available for conferees).  Finally, some conferees speculated that whatever the present level of female threat activity, with the general liberation of women in the United States, threats from women are likely to increase in the future.***

---

*Milton Eisenhower et al., To Establish Justice, To Insure Domestic Tranquility, Final Report of the National Commission on the Causes and Prevention of Violence (Washington, D. C.:  U. S. Government Printing Office, 1969), pp. 122-24.

**The conference was concluded prior to the attempt on President Reagan's life by John W. Hinckley, Jr., on March 30, 1981.
     Lynette ("Squeaky") Fromme attempted to assassinate President Ford on September 5, 1975, in Sacramento, California; and Sara Jane Moore attempted to assassinate President Ford on September 22, 1975, in San Francisco, California.

***See paper by Frazier and colleagues, page 93, for fuller treatment of the issue of female assassins.

As with women, the Secret Service caseload of blacks, Hispanics, and other minorities is increasing. Because minority groups have become politically visible and vocal in recent years, conferees thought the Secret Service should anticipate a higher level of threat activity from such groups in the future.

## Terrorists

Conferees echoed the worldwide concern over terrorism. From the point of view of daily Secret Service operations, however, agent responses to dangers from terrorist conspiracies are very different from their typical evaluative activities with emotionally unstable threateners. A different type of judgment is used in assessing and responding to dangerousness of a terrorist group; in such a situation, the Secret Service (along with other government agencies) employs procedures more like those of a criminal investigation, rather than the usual protective intelligence evaluation which includes assessing many personal and psychosocial factors.*

## Political Dissidents

Charles Halpern, among others, raised the possibility that persons and groups having specific political grievances or policy disagreements with government leaders may engage in violence to achieve their goals. Such persons would be drawn from populations quite different than the populations from which the mentally disturbed cases with which the Secret Service is presently so heavily concerned are drawn.

## Other Sources of Danger to Protected Leaders

As many conferees observed, public appearances by protected leaders in certain situations and settings may enhance their risk of attack from persons and groups with sinister intent. Some risk to their lives may also be brought about by the behaviors of the protected leaders themselves.**

Problems in predicting whether and when an individual might engage in behavior harmful to a protected person, coupled with the many difficulties and dilemmas associated with monitoring and

_____

*See memorandum by Jenkins, page 177.

**Presentations by David Hamburg and Walter Menninger are relevant here, as is Saleem Shah's paper (pages 13, 147, and 121, respectively).

otherwise managing subjects identified as dangerous (to be discussed below), make it essential that other means of minimizing risk to protected persons be explored.

## Situations and Settings That Enhance Risk

Several conferees suggested that the Secret Service analyze situations and settings in terms of the level of risk they may pose to protected leaders. Public appearances of protected persons in particular geographic areas may be inherently dangerous, and certain types of situations and settings may be relatively easy to penetrate or present unusual difficulties for Secret Service protective units. For instance, appearances of protected figures among large and excited crowds, such as at national political conventions, enhance risk no matter how much security is provided. Similarly, the volume of threats may be higher during presidential campaigns and periods of national crisis or emergency, making alternative or special protective strategies advisable.

One suggestion, proposed by Patricia Wald, was to analyze the situations in which assassinations and assassination attempts have occurred, both in the United S*ates and abroad, to determine which of them might be likely sources of future risk to American government leaders (and visiting dignitaries, when protected). Such a study, which could be approached historically, might include examination of the concept of "defensible space" and investigate the methods of successful and would-be assassins.

Charles Whitebread suggested that there may be relatively simple technological devices already in existence or soon to be developed that could greatly assist the Service in its task of situational protection. Such devices might include physical barriers or metal detectors installed along parade routes and at other entry points to areas where public appearances of protected persons are scheduled.

A third suggestion was to examine fluctuations in the volume of threats to protected persons in relation to political and public events, the behaviors of the protected, and other situational or environmental factors deemed relevant, in order to plan appropriate defensive strategies during empirically determined periods of high risk.*

_____

*Franklin Zimring's memorandum, page 183, is relevant here.

## General Availability of Weapons

Conferees noted that the ready availability of weapons in the United States is a factor that must be emphasized in any discussion of violence, however naive or unsophisticated it may appear to restate the obvious.

There was no question, in the opinion of conferees or Secret Service representatives, that weapons availability substantially enhances the risk of harm to protected persons. Intelligence investigations of Secret Service subjects always inquire into weapons knowledge and possession, but the Service is virtually powerless to control a dangerous subject's access to weapons. This fact was illustrated by a Secret Service case presentation about a person who acquired a gun promptly after being discharged from a mental hospital and, while supposedly en route to another mental hospital in a different state, shot and killed a Secret Service agent.

Conferees said that the problem of weapons availability must be resolved through the political process, and conceded that an extensive discussion of alternative remedies was beyond the scope of the conference. They also felt that present federal legislation prohibiting the sale of weapons to persons who have been convicted of a felony or are "mentally defective" is insufficiently broad and inadequately enforced. They supported a suggestion by John Lion that any subject who has been judged dangerous by the Secret Service should be barred from access to weapons.

## Behaviors of Protected Persons

Do protected leaders behave in ways that facilitate attempts on their lives? Are some leaders "danger prone"? These questions were briefly entertained in plenary and workshop discussions, and are addressed more fully in presentations by David Hamburg and W. Walter Menninger, and in Saleem Shah's paper.

Some conferees suggested that protected persons, particularly presidents, may contribute to attempts on their lives by deliberately exposing themselves to situations of high risk--for instance mingling in crowds and "pressing the flesh." Hamburg commented that presidents, presidential candidates, and other elected leaders say they want to mix with ordinary citizens for two reasons: to demonstrate that they do and can interact meaningfully with the rank-and-file and not just with elites; and to create opportunities for the public to explore their knowledge, views, and skills, and ultimately to test their qualifications to hold high office. Other conferees suggested that less lofty motivations, perhaps shared by many celebrities and public figures, may underlie this risk-taking behavior.

Limiting the Exposure of Protected Leaders

Though most of their attention and energies were directed elsewhere, some conferees briefly touched upon possible ways to limit the exposure of presidents and other protected persons to potentially dangerous situations. Hamburg, for instance, suggested that there may be equally effective, though more sheltered, settings in which such leaders can achieve the dual goals cited above.* Several conferees, and Secret Service representatives as well, however, thought it might be difficult to convince public leaders that they should refrain from the types of exposure they may feel are important. Robert Michels observed that "it is going to remain the Service's problem of maximizing the protection within the domain of freedom that we allocate our leaders." Nevertheless, Michels and several others shared the view that protected leaders might be induced to modify their behavior if "mandated" to do so by other authorities and if in so doing they did not give the appearance of personal cowardice. "As long as it comes from outside what is [perceived as] their choice--something imposed on them--it takes away the politically negative connotations," Michels commented. In this connection, it was proposed that protected leaders--at least the most visible of them--wear bullet-proof vests during public appearances. A more radical suggestion was that federal legislation be developed to limit the freedom of movement of protected leaders, the requirements of which would be imposed in such a way as to enable them to avoid the appearance of cowardliness.


SUGGESTED APPROACHES TO THE STUDY OF ASSASSINATION


Many types of violence and violent persons have been extensively studied and are well understood, but the phenomenon of assassination is not among them. In contrast to many other violent crimes, assassination occurs very rarely--at least in the United States--which means that there are few instances available for study. Infrequent, or low "base rate," events present special problems for those who would like to be able to predict their occurrence and design research to expand knowledge about the conditions under which they occur and the kinds of persons likely to be engaged in them. The infrequency of assassination, especially assassination of those protected by the Secret Service, is of course, both encouraging and highly desirable. At the same time, however, the low incidence of this behavior has made it very difficult for the

---

*See also Saleem Shah's paper, page 121.

44

Secret Service to learn whether its own information-gathering
activities and interventions with persons considered potentially
dangerous are appropriately targeted and have any validity.  As
Alfred Blumstein pointed out, the Secret Service has had a great deal
of experience with threats, threateners, and a variety of untoward
behaviors presumed to be indicative of impending assassination
attempts (if intervention is not forthcoming), but very little
experience with assassination itself.*

In both plenary and workshop sessions, conference participants
and Secret Service representatives alike raised many questions about
the characteristics and possible motivations of potential assassins,
as represented by the caseload of subjects the Secret Service
considers potentially dangerous to those it protects.  John Monahan
mentioned three frequently cited motivations for assassination:  the
desire to murder one's father through killing a symbolic father (in
the person of the president, for instance), the desire to attain
glory by killing of a famous person, and the desire to commit suicide
in the process of killing another.  Many had questions about victim
selection:  why one person is targeted for assassination rather than
another.  To what extent, participants wanted to know, are victims
interchangeable?  If a subject expresses a direction of interest
toward one protected person (the president, for example), might that
subject also be dangerous to other protected persons (the vice
president or the president's wife, for instance)?  In the same vein,
if a subject expresses hostile intent toward a senator, governor, or
mayor, is that subject also a risk to persons protected by the Secret
Service?  Similarly, if a subject threatens to harm a protected
person, might that subject also, or alternatively, harm a Secret
Service agent?**  And if a subject is known to have had sinister
intent toward a past president of the United States, should he or she
also be considered a risk to the current president?  Conferees also
wondered whether persons with hostile intent toward non-political
public figures might evidence similar hostility toward political
leaders.  For example, are people who threaten or harm celebrity
figures likely to be dangerous toward persons the Secret Service
protects?

---

*For discussion of some methodological and substantive problems
associated with low base rate behaviors, see presentations by James
Billings, Don Gottfredson, Jenkins, and Monahan (pages 143, 139, 145,
and 129, respectively); and memoranda by Jenkins, Monahan, and
Zimring (pages 177, 179, and 183, respectively).

**This concern was prompted by a Secret Service case
presentation involving a subject who had expressed animosity toward
protected persons and subsequently killed a Secret Service agent.

A somewhat different and more basic issue touched upon earlier was raised by Marvin Wolfgang, who wanted to know the relationship between threats and actions. Are those who have thus far done nothing more than threaten a protected person likely to follow through on their threats, or are threateners and actors two distinct groups? Speculating on the motivations of persons who engage in extortion threats with which he is familiar, Jenkins noted that four patterns have been identified: those for whom threatening itself is a form of gratification and constitutes expressive behavior, and who have no interest in carrying out their threats; those who hope, by threatening, to disrupt normal activities and create chaos; those who are interested in extorting money or goods, but not in carrying out the threatened activity; and those who have a genuine interest in carrying out the threatened activity itself and can not be bought off.

In view of the many unknowns, conferees suggested that the Secret Service would benefit from empirical studies designed to increase its understanding of assassination, and thereby to improve its ability to detect those who may be truly dangerous to persons it protects. The following ideas for research were proposed, some of them as methods of expanding the number of cases available for study:

## Comparison of Dangerous and Never-Dangerous Cases

On the assumption that the Secret Service itself is the best judge of the level of risk posed by subjects to persons it protects, several conferees suggested that a retrospective analysis and comparison of dangerous and never dangerous subjects in its files would probably be a good starting point for understanding the characteristics of potential assassins.

## Study of Behaviors Similar to Assassination

Because assassination is so rare--at least in the United States--and the Secret Service caseload of subjects contains no one who has ever attempted it, several conferees suggested that the Service try to test the validity of its own decision-making with respect to dangerousness on a similar, or "proxy," behavior that occurs with some frequency among its caseload of subjects. The validity of agent predictions (dangerous or not dangerous) would be tested by examining the extent to which these predictions correctly distinguish subjects who do and do not subsequently engage in the proxy behavior.

This idea was originally proposed by Franklin Zimring and is discussed in his memorandum circulated to conferees and included in this report.*  In that memorandum, Zimring suggested acts of personal violence toward strangers and suicide as possible "proxies" on which to test the validity of agent decision-making.  Although neither of these was considered truly parallel to assassination, several conferees thought their incidence among Secret Service cases might be worth examining.  Others, however, had reservations about the use of suicide as a proxy, even though an empirical connection between homicide and suicide has often been observed, and clinicians have noted similarities in the psychodynamics underlying both behaviors.  James Billings, an expert in suicide research, did not support the use of suicide as a proxy for assassination, though he did think there were similar methodological problems in identifying likely candidates for each type of behavior.**  Conferees also suspected that the incidence of suicide among cases on file with the Secret Service might be too low to yield valid results.

## Study of "Threshold" Behaviors of Secret Service Subjects

Assassination and attempted assassination are rare, but there must be many instances, as Charles Halpern observed, in which a Secret Service subject or other person has come very close to making an assassination attempt, but was deflected by Secret Service agents or others just as he or she was on the threshold of so doing.***  Halpern suggested that "threshold" behaviors--immediate preludes to assassination attempts--be carefully analyzed and described to better understand behavioral indicators of imminent danger and detect possible flaws in the Secret Service protective system.  Such a study could be begun by asking special agents to recall their "near misses."

## Detailed Study of Assassins

Walter Menninger suggested that a detailed study of all assassins and attempted assassins of political leaders, whether living or dead, should be undertaken.  Such a study should include descriptive and clinical data on the personalities and backgrounds

---

*See page 183.  A member of the planning committee, Zimring was unable to attend the conference.
  Also relevant in this connection are memoranda by Gable and Monahan, pages 171 and 179, respectively.

**See presentation by Billings, page 143.

***One such case was described by a Secret Service representative at a planning committee meeting prior to the conference.

of these persons, as well as the circumstances surrounding their attempted or successful assaults.

## Clinical Studies of Attackers of Prominent Persons

To increase the number of cases available for scrutiny, several conferees suggested that persons who have attacked or attempted to attack prominent political figures other than, or in addition to, those protected by the Secret Service might be studied. Such targets could include elected leaders, such as senators, congressmen, governors, mayors; appointed officials; and/or prominent activists, such as civil rights leaders. Such a study might be limited to the United States, or might include attempted and successful assassins of foreign leaders in their own countries. Alternatively, or in addition, persons who have attacked or attempted to assault famous persons or celebrity figures other than political leaders might be studied. Edwin Megargee suggested that such a study might include an assessment of the personality patterns of those who engage in such behaviors and the skills required to carry them out. It might also be possible, as Wolfgang suggested, to examine the level and type of threat activity which preceded such attacks and compare those who have given prior notice with those who have not.

## Studies in Victim Provocation

Sara Eddy suggested it might be useful to examine whether there is anything specific about political leaders themselves—their personalities, political style, the nature of their public statements, and so forth—which might elicit threats to their safety or assaults on their lives. She suggested that a sample of political leaders who have been threatened be compared with a sample who have never been threatened.

In a similar vein, Elissa Benedek suggested that those presidents who have had the most threats on their lives be examined to see whether anything about their personalities, style, or behavior could be considered provocative to would-be assassins.

## RELATIONSHIP BETWEEN THE SECRET SERVICE
## AND THE MENTAL HEALTH COMMUNITY

Because approximately 90 percent of the subjects whom Secret Service special agents presently consider dangerous had been previously diagnosed as having mental or emotional disturbances, conferees explored current and possible future relationships between the Secret Service and mental health professionals.

Based on pre-conference briefings by Secret Service personnel and conference discussion, many participants—especially psychiatrists and other clinicians—felt that the present relationship between the Secret Service and the mental health community is inadequate in magnitude and less than optimal in terms of overall quality. The Secret Service is not at present a fully informed consumer of mental health services.

As with other topics of discussion, conferees stressed that implementation of their suggestions or ideas for improvements might result in incremental gains, but not in great improvements. They also hoped that the mental health aspects of the Secret Service assessment and management tasks would not deflect attention from other equally or perhaps more important aspects of Secret Service operations.

### Current Methods of Dealing with Mentally Ill Subjects

Because so many of its dangerous subjects seem to have mental or emotional problems, the Secret Service itself acts as both a provider and consumer of mental health services. The Service provides mental health services to the extent that it operates as a kind of emergency mental health facility for disturbed subjects whose behavior is bizarre or otherwise apparently dangerous to protected persons and for whom it is unable to obtain assistance from mental health personnel and institutions. In these instances, Secret Service special agents must often "babysit" such subjects, try to help them, and otherwise take responsibility for monitoring their whereabouts until outside assistance can be enlisted, if at all. The Service acts as a consumer of mental health services to the extent that it (1) uses its few informal ad hoc relationships with various mental hospitals and clinicians for consultation about difficult cases, (2) facilitates hospital admissions for subjects it considers highly dangerous to protected persons, (3) monitors the progress of subjects based on information provided from hospital personnel, and (4) arranges follow-up psychiatric care for its non-institutionalized subjects.

When mental illness is suspected as the underlying cause of a subject's dangerous statements or behaviors, Secret Service agents typically try to convince the subject to admit himself, on a voluntary basis, to a mental hospital for observation and evaluation. Agents often prefer this management route because it gets the subject off the street. As some conferees pointed out, however, voluntary admission is at best only a temporary solution, because the subject will typically be evaluated and released within 10 to 20 days, when he or she will again become the full responsibility of the Secret Service in its protective function.* Second, because the Secret Service has peace officer status in only eight states,** involuntary commitment (for apparently mentally ill subjects who refuse or are unable to admit themselves voluntarily) requires the active involvement and cooperation of local police, family members and/or psychiatrists, and is far from routine. (The decision to commit an individual for emergency observation is, of course, a medical one, and not a Secret Service function.) Additionally, though hospital personnel are asked and expected by the Secret Service to alert the Service when one of its subjects is about to be discharged, special agents have found they cannot rely on them to do so.

## Obstacles to Professional Relationship

Both Secret Service representatives and conferees--particularly clinicians--felt that at present there are several obstacles to the establishment of mutually beneficial relationships between the Secret Service and the mental health community. These are rooted in conflicting values and differences in orientation, function, and professional training and experience.

## Differences in Values, Orientation, and Function

Although Secret Service agents and mental health professionals may in many instances be dealing with the same person, or with similar populations (e.g., the mentally ill or emotionally disturbed), their professional orientation toward such clients or subjects will necessarily differ. For example, psychiatrists

---

*See also Management of Dangerous Subjects, page 59.

**The following is a generally accepted definition of the term "peace officer": "any person who, by virtue of his/her office or public employment, is vested by law with a duty to maintain public order or to make arrest for offenses while acting within the scope of his/her authority." The Secret Service has peace officer status in Alaska, Hawaii, Idaho, Kansas, Montana, Utah, Virginia, Wisconsin, and the District of Columbia.

are concerned primarily with treatment and establishing a therapeutic alliance with the patient, which is usually enhanced by the ethic of confidentiality and the privileged nature of most doctor-patient communications. The Secret Service, in contrast, must deal with subjects within the context of social control, law enforcement, and criminal justice, however much special agents may also be interested in promoting the personal welfare of such persons. To some extent, differences in values, orientation, and functions hinder the development of cooperative relationships between the Secret Service and the mental health community, as some members of each may have negative images of the other. For example, some psychiatrists view Secret Service agents as cops who practice deceit, and whose intervention may render successful treatment of their patients an impossibility. Many psychiatrists, in fact, would be reluctant to violate the confidential relationship they have with their patients in order to oblige Secret Service requests for information. Similarly, Secret Service agents may view psychiatrists and other mental health professionals as uncooperative and unnecessarily reticent about those of their patients who are, or could become, Secret Service subjects by virtue of threatening a protected person. Secret Service representatives also mentioned difficulties they have encountered in obtaining information from hospital records about subjects who have threatened protected persons or otherwise behaved in ways considered dangerous to them. In their view, concern with the rights of patients--and with civil liberties generally--has increased in the past few years, making their ability to carry out their protective duties much more difficult.

As amply illustrated in both plenary and workshop discussions, each side also recognizes the danger of co-optation by the other, if the working relationships between the Secret Service and the mental health community were to be improved. The inadvisability and potential hazards of either side wearing two hats were extensively discussed.


Basis for Mutually Beneficial Relationships

Despite the gravity of the obstacles discussed above, many conferees felt that a framework for mutually productive relationships between the Secret Service and the mental health community could be developed. Adherence to the following precepts was considered essential to the establishment of successful relationships:

● Ideally, there should be no role confusion or blurring of the distinction between the appropriate role of the Secret Service and that of the mental health professions. In John Lion's opinion, each group must recognize a "fundamental division . . . between

police types of work and clinical practitioner types of efforts."
That is, Secret Service agents must at all times be realistically
aware of their own goals (for instance, to do what they deem
necessary to protect the president from potentially dangerous
persons), while mental health professionals must similarly give their
full allegiance to the credo of their professions (for example, to do
what is in the best interest of the patient or client, from a
therapeutic standpoint). In short, relationships between the Secret
Service and the mental health community should be built on
"cooperation without co-optation."

   ● Neither the Secret Service nor the mental health community
can delegate its own responsibilities to the other. The Secret
Service, for instance, cannot assume that if it turns a subject over
to the mental health system for evaluation, treatment, and/or
monitoring, its responsibility for that subject in relation to its
protective function has ended.* Secret Service agents should
themselves be prepared to interview subjects in the hospital, if and
when they are hospitalized. Likewise, mental health professionals
cannot delegate medical decisions (for instance, determination as to
whether a subject is committable to a hospital for observation) to
Secret Service personnel.

   ● To develop mutually satisfactory relationships between the
Secret Service and the mental health community, each must learn more
about what the other does, how it is done, and what each other's
competencies and limitations are.

   ● Such relationships as are developed should be based on the
principle of collegiality. There should be less deference on the
part of the Secret Service to the presumed expertise and superior
wisdom of psychiatric opinion, for instance.


Formal and Informal Relationships

   Conferees reached no conclusion as to whether relationships
between the Secret Service and mental health practitioners and
institutions should be kept informal (the way they are at present) or
formalized into more permanent, standing arrangements whereby the
Secret Service would contract for specific services from particular
institutions and mental health professionals over a period of time.

---

   *The Secret Service does not presently delegate that
responsibility, nor does it anticipate wanting or being able to do so.

John Lion argued against formalizing the relationships, because he feared that the mental health professionals and institutions involved would run a serious risk of co-optation by Secret Service goals and the professional integrity of the psychiatric community would thereby be compromised. A non-institutionalized ad hoc consultation process, he felt, would be much less likely to result in co-optation. Such an approach would mean that the Secret Service would consult various different practitioners or institutions on a one-time or infrequent basis, but not repeatedly over long periods of time. Several other conferees, however, noting the less than optimal quality of some of the advice and consultation the Secret Service presently receives and the inadequacies in patient care provided to some of its subjects, thought it would be advantageous to the Service to know and develop continuing relationships with specific mental health practitioners and institutional providers in the geographic areas where the largest numbers of dangerous subjects are typically found. Formal agreements or written understandings with competent professionals and institutions would improve the overall quality of the assistance the Secret Service receives in the mental health field. Joseph English suggested that liasons with specific teaching hospitals having a major psychiatric capacity would be a useful way of providing the Secret Service with first-rate advice and consultation.

## Some Proposals for Establishing Linkages

Many different proposals or models for establishing productive relationships between the Secret Service and the mental health community were suggested by conferees. Each of the suggestions below would be one method by which the Service could enhance its capacity for decision-making with respect to its caseload of mentally or emotionally disturbed subjects.

● The Secret Service might solicit the advice of psychiatrists when dealing with difficult or ambiguous cases, where there is some question as to the subject's diagnosis and prognosis, with implications for dangerousness to the protected person.

● Rather than use the services of mental health consultants whose allegiance is external to the Service, the Secret Service could hire its own mental health experts or psychiatrists as staff members, whose role would be defined by the Service's mission.

● The informal consulting relationship that has recently been developed between the Boston field office of the Secret Service and the McLean-Bridgewater Program of Belmont, Massachusetts, might serve as a prototype for the development of similar relationships elsewhere in the country. This cooperative arrangement enables Secret Service field office personnel to learn about psychiatric disorders and their relationship to dangerousness, and to observe clinicians interviewing violent patients (with the informed consent of such patients).*

● A nationwide network of local mental health resource centers could be developed to provide the Secret Service with consultation and advice in screening incoming cases for relevancy, assessing potentially dangerous subjects, and handling the disposition of cases. Consultants to such centers might include representatives from the criminal justice system, mental health professionals, civil libertarians, and others whose expertise and concerns are relevant to the Secret Service mission.** One Secret Service representative had reservations about this proposal because he felt it might involve unwarranted delegation of Secret Service authority and responsibilities to an outside reviewing body.

## Constraints on Mental Health Provider Capacities

Although the Service could undoubtedly benefit from the advice and assistance of mental health professionals and institutions in the area of assessing and managing dangerous subjects, clinicians cautioned Secret Service representatives not to overestimate the capacity of the mental health system to respond. They emphasized that mental health facilities are undergoing major changes in underlying philosophy, staffing patterns, and funding, especially with respect to the chronically mentally ill, who are being sent back into their communities in great numbers. Cutbacks in institutional services to the chronically mentally ill are causing hardships for other institutions and organizations, as they try to absorb and provide services to this population that until recently was relatively confined. Some conferees noted that the Secret Service may in some measure be heir to the deinstitutionalization of the chronically mentally ill, as many of the Service's problem subjects (including repeat threateners) seem to come from this population. Because of such policy changes in the mental health field, clinicians told Secret Service representatives to expect that it will become increasingly difficult for the Service to have its subjects either committed to mental hospitals for observation and evaluation, or to gain long-term institutional care for subjects who are chronically mentally ill. Rather, the Service should be prepared to look to management alternatives other than long- or short-term commitment to mental hospitals.

---

*For fuller details, see paper by Frazier and colleagues, page 93.

**For fuller elaboration of this concept, see paper by Shervert Frazier and colleagues.

## Legal and Ethical Issues in the Relationships

There are many unresolved and thorny legal and ethical issues in the current and possible future relationships between the Secret Service and the mental health community. A number of these were raised or touched upon during the conference, but most are in need of further study and clarification, as discussed below.

### Issues of Confidentiality and Privacy

To what extent do and should psychiatrists and other mental health professionals report to the Secret Service threats against protected persons which they might hear from patients? This issue was provocatively raised in a commissioned paper by Robert Michels, included in this volume.* In that paper, Michels asks why it is that there are so few referrals from the psychiatric community to the Secret Service.

The legal and ethical issues involved here are complex and will not be readily resolved to the satisfaction of interested parties--principally psychiatrists, patients/subjects, and the Secret Service. Three points of law are involved. First, under federal statute 18 USC 871, the so-called "threat statute," it is a felony to make a threat against the president of the United States. Theoretically, anyone who witnesses such a threat is obligated to report it to the Secret Service; failure to do so constitutes misprision of a felony.** Second, the traditional confidentiality and privileged status of the doctor-patient relationship is often but variously codified in state law. As noted by Alan Stone, the extent to which such confidentiality is protected in practice is complicated by the fact that "different states treat the confidentiality of patients differently . . . ."*** The third is the "duty to protect" issue, sometimes referred to as the "duty to warn" stemming from civil law and its extention into the psychotherapist-patient relationship. This principle was preeminently highlighted in the 1976 California Supreme Court decision in Tarasoff v. Regents

---

*See page 107.

**Under Title 18, USC, Section 4, a misprision of a felony occurs when a person "having knowledge of the actual commission of a felony recognizable by a court of the United States, conceals and does not as soon as possible make known the same to some judge or other person in civil or military authority under the United States."

***Memorandum from Alan A. Stone to Institute of Medicine staff, May 6, 1981. Dr. Stone, a member of the planning committee, was unable to attend the conference.

of the University of California, which stated, "When a therapist determines, or pursuant to the standards of his profession, should determine, that his patients presents a serious danger of violence to another, he incurs an obligation to use reasonable care to protect the intended victim against such danger."* How much this ruling potentially undermines the therapeutic alliance between the doctor and patient and is in conflict with the confidentiality tradition is a matter of debate. One conferee, psychiatrist Frank Ochberg, observed, "We are in the business of serving the individual client and not the state, but we are beginning to be held somehow responsible, culpable, for the dangerous delusions of some of our patients." Stone contends that "the decision to protect the community and reveal confidences is clearly and obviously ethical. The failing of the ethical code is that it gives no guidance as to what degree of danger justifies the decision.** There has additionally been concern in the psychiatric community about liability for breaking confidence in order to protect or warn. Stone contends that although therapists may be "troubled" about breaking confidence, "the canons of ethics for psychiatry permit this and the reality seems to be that there would be little genuine risk of civil liability unless the therapist is quite irresponsible in evaluating the danger posed by his patient." If a patient were to sue, Stone maintains, "the legal claim must be that the therapist was negligent in diagnosing the patient as dangerous. That should be as difficult to prove as that the patient was not dangerous."***

Michels himself noted, in workshop, that there is no obligation to report distant threats. In all likelihood, most psychiatrists would base their reporting decisions on their own estimates of the patient's imminent dangerousness to a potential victim. Secret Service personnel say, however, that they themselves would like to be in a position to evaluate the seriousness of such threats (and the dangerousness of the threateners), and therefore would want to be informed when such threats occur. (The ethical aspect of this question is independent of the quality control consequences of a vastly increased Secret Service caseload that might result if such reporting became widespread.)

How much, if any, information about a psychiatric patient who is also a Secret Service subject should be shared between mental health professionals and Secret Service personnel, and who should do

---

*Tarasoff v. Regents of the University of California, 17 Cal. 3d at 431, 551 P.2d at 340, 131 Cal. Rptr. at 20.

**Stone, op. cit.

***Stone, op. cit.

the sharing?  Should there be some uniform practices or requirements concerning the sharing of information about a patient/subject between mental health professionals and institutions on the one hand and the Secret Service on the other?  Secret Service personnel say they are hampered in their investigations by variations in state law as to their access to hospital records.

If the Secret Service uses psychiatric consultants to assist in assessing and monitoring Secret Service subjects, would it be ethical for such consultants (a) to render judgments on subjects they have not personally interviewed, and/or (b) to consult about the subject with a psychiatrist who has first-hand knowledge about the subject, in order to advise the Secret Service concerning the subject's likely dangerousness or an appropriate monitoring strategy?  That is, could and should a Secret Service psychiatric consultant render an opinion on a subject without having evaluated the subject?

## Issues of Professional Independence in Judgment

The possibility that mental health professionals might be co-opted by Secret Service goals has already been mentioned as an issue some clinicians thought worthy of attention.  The subject was broached most directly in the presentation by Joseph English.*  Conferees emphasized, for instance, that decisions involving emergency admissions of persons to hospitals for psychiatric evaluation are legally and appropriately medical decisions, and not ones that should be made directly or indirectly by Secret Service personnel.  The desire to be helpful to the Secret Service in its task of protecting government leaders should not overshadow professional medical judgment about admitting a subject to a hospital for evaluation.

### Some Suggestions for Study and Clarification

R. K. Gable suggested, and others concurred, that the controversial legal and ethical issues in the relationship between the Secret Service and the mental health community should be clarified and guidelines for Secret Service procedures and conduct developed.  Among these issues are:

● confidentiality of information revealed in psychiatric interviews versus the obligation to protect a potential victim

● liability of clinicians for errors of judgment with respect to Secret Service subjects

---

*See page 155.

● legality of imposing certain requirements on mental patients as a condition of their release from hospitals, similar to probation requirements for persons released from prison (such as non-possession of firearms).

Gable also suggested that the Secret Service's manual of legal opinions and decisions be reviewed by mental health attorneys and mental health administrators.

Robert Michels made the following suggestions: (1) that a dialogue among mental health professionals concerning the legal and ethical dilemmas in the relationship between the Secret Service and the mental health community be initiated; (2) that there be consideration of regulations and laws to protect from liability professionals who warn in good faith, analogous to the protection provided for the reporting of child abuse; (3) that policies be developed to assure that the Secret Service consider not only the "rights" of subjects, but also their "interests," in order to reassure mental health professionals that it is appropriate for them to warn when indicated; (4) that mental health professionals be made aware of the fact that a threat against the president is a felony and therefore the threshold for warning is different from what it might be for threats against other persons; and (5) that a procedure to collect and study warnings received from mental health professionals under the threat statute be established.*

Two new federal statutes were also proposed, but neither was discussed in depth. Joseph English thought a federal commitment statute should replace the individual state commitment statutes, which are confusing in their non-uniformity with respect to commitment criteria. In connection with discussion of malpractice and hospital liability insurance, John Monahan suggested that a statute with the provision that the federal goverment assume liability for activities undertaken by a mental health professional in conjunction with the Secret Service might be useful. R. K. Gable suggested that the various state mental health statutes and regulations be reviewed and the most compatible ones used as the basis for developing draft (federal) statutes and regulations. Charles Halpern was opposed to the creation of any new statutes which would enhance the powers of the Secret Service.

---

*Memorandum from Robert Michels to Institute of Medicine staff, June 1, 1981.

## MANAGEMENT OF DANGEROUS SUBJECTS

If a subject is determined by the Secret Service to be potentially dangerous to one or more protected persons, he or she is placed on "quarterly investigation." The quarterly investigation procedure involves reinterviewing the subject and/or others no later than three months from the time of the previous investigation, updating the information on file, and deciding again whether the subject is dangerous or not dangerous. In many instances, however, subjects considered dangerous are investigated and/or monitored more frequently. Each time a subject is evaluated as dangerous, he or she is scheduled for a quarterly investigation until such time as the agents decide he or she is no longer dangerous. Based on the findings of initial and subsequent investigations, decisions also are made about the disposition of the case. Examples of such dispositions include referring the subject to a hospital for psychiatric evaluation, attempting to prosecute the subject for violation of the threat statute, or allowing the subject to remain on the street while agents monitor his whereabouts and activities. Whether or not the disposition results in the subject's confinement, the three-month reevaluation requirement still holds.

At any one time, 250 to 400 subjects are on quarterly investigation. The number of so-called QI's varies from day to day, as new cases are added and old (no longer dangerous) cases are dropped. The size of the QI caseload at any particular time depends on many factors, and has been observed to vary with political conditions, national and international events, and the extent to which protected persons—particularly the president—are in the public eye. For instance, during the campaign period preceding a presidential election, and at the beginning of a new president's first term in office, the list is apt to be somewhat larger than normal. Actual assassination attempts on the life of a president also tend to be followed by an increase in the number of threats or other potentially dangerous activity, much of which comes from new subjects.

Subjects particularly worrisome to the Service are those whose hostile interest in a protected person is high and intense, and who are not presently confined in a penal or mental institution. Secret Service concern about a subject is also heightened if he or she happens to live in the Washington, D. C., area (where a large number of protected persons are in residence), or when a protected person visits the subject's area of residence. In order to insure the safety of those it protects, the Service tries to minimize the opportunities for dangerous subjects to come in contact with protected persons, and does so by monitoring their whereabouts and status very carefully or, if appropriate, by resorting to the mental health or criminal justice system to secure their confinement. For instance, for subjects who seem mentally disturbed and have made serious threats against a protected person, or who have behaved in other ways considered potentially dangerous to such persons, agents will often attempt to arrange their admission to a mental institution either voluntarily or involuntarily. For subjects who, by all indications, are not mentally ill but who, in the opinion of the Service, have violated the threat statute, special agents will often try for prosecution and incarceration under 18 USC 871.

## Intervention: Some General Considerations

Conferees were in substantial agreement on the following points:

1. The goal of all intervention with subjects is to reduce the level of danger they present to protected persons. In that task, the Secret Service should use the least restrictive alternatives and benign interventions wherever possible. That is, the Service should try to discover and use the least damaging, least coercive, and least intrusive intervention measures consistent with the level of apparent danger posed by the subject. Adherence to this principle should preclude confrontations with subjects who may otherwise feel their civil rights have been violated.

2. Management options should be carefully examined and compared in terms of their effectiveness and cost. Alternatives that are sufficiently effective and least costly should be selected, provided they also meet the least restrictive criterion. Several conferees, for example, suggested that frequent telephone contact with subjects might be just as effective as an interview, and yet be far less costly.

3. Instruments used in reassessing QI subjects should be capable of yielding high quality information as to the subject's current mental and emotional status, level of interest in protected persons, and ability to carry out untoward acts.

4. Although the Secret Service seeks to control its subjects' violence potential toward protected persons, interventions need not have an adverse effect on subjects. In some cases they may well be therapeutic and thus of benefit to the subject as well as the protected person.

5. While there is no firm evidence that intervention with potentially dangerous subjects really is a deterrent to violence, the Secret Service cannot afford to test the effectiveness of its activities by suspending its interventions on a trial basis, because the risk of assassination is unacceptable. The most the Service can do is test the relative effectiveness of alternatiave intervention strategies.

## Observations on Present Case Management Practices

Descriptions of the quarterly investigation process and the dispositional strategies typically used by Secret Service agents led many conferees to conclude that the Service is at times insufficiently flexible to achieve its goals effectively and efficiently. More effective management strategies might eliminate the need for improving predictive accuracy--the extent to which dangerous and not dangerous decisions are the correct ones.

Some conferees noted that present intervention strategies seem to be geared toward short-term rather than long-term solutions, with the result that subjects who are neutralized or otherwise effectively handled for the time being are likely to reappear as dangerous at some later date. For example, subjects temporarily incapacitated by virtue of having been sent to a hospital for a 48-hour psychiatric evaluation are likely to pose problems for the Service when discharged.

In the opinion of several clinicians, management procedures should be tailored to meet the particular problems presented by each individual case, rather than standardized for use with all subjects. The task in monitoring or managing subjects, as in the management of psychiatric patients, is to determine "the optimal series of individual [management] decisions" for each subject, according to Robert Michels. Management strategies should also, of course, vary according to the anticipated proximity between a subject and his or her target. One method might be appropriate when a protected person is scheduled to visit a subject's area of residence, while another would be more useful when the subject is separated from the protected person by considerable physical distance. Similarly, monitoring strategies with subjects already confined should probably be different from those used with subjects on the street. For subjects who reside in areas where many protected individuals live (such as in the metropolitan Washington, D. C., area) still other tactics might be particularly appropriate. The Secret Service is, of course, sensitive to the need to vary its monitoring strategies in accordance with the situation and the particulars of the case, and in fact does so. Conferees simply wanted to encourage the Service to expand its efforts along these lines and to explore a broader range of tactics than it now uses.

Some conferees questioned whether the current practice of dropping in on subjects in their homes on an unannounced basis for an interview is the most effective way to elicit the information needed. Alternative suggestions here were to conduct interviews in Secret Service field offices or to make appointments for interviews in subjects' homes.

In the opinion of several conferees, reevaluation or reassessment of a dangerous subject at periodic intervals should be undertaken not so much for the purpose of determining whether or not he or she is still dangerous, but rather to decide whether, in comparison with the last evaluation, the subject is becoming more or less dangerous. Two separate assessments are necessary here: a decision as to whether the subject's mental status is improving or worsening (requiring agents to be able to detect slight shifts in functioning), and a decision as to whether the subject is becoming more or less lethal (i.e., moving from verbal hostility toward hostile action, or vice versa). Agents should be aware that a short-term improvement in mental status does not necessarily imply that the subject poses less risk to protected persons.

## Case Management through the Criminal Justice System

For subjects the Secret Service considers to be in violation of the threat statute (18 USC 871), special agents often attempt prosecution. However, the proportion of cases actually prosecuted (and convicted) under the statute is relatively low, apparently because many such threats are viewed by United States attorneys and the courts as constituting the legitimate exercise of free speech, or simply verbal hyperbole. Conferees noted this fact and did not explore it.*

## Case Management through the Mental Health System

Case management of mentally disturbed or psychotic individuals with a history of violence, or who are considered potentially violent, was discussed by Menninger in his presentation (Part III, "Some Techniques for Managing Potentially Violent Individuals"), and by Shervert Frazier in his presentation on interviewing techniques to be used for assessing potentially dangerous subjects.

As previously mentioned, when a subject's threats or dangerous behaviors are viewed as manifestations of mental or emotional illness, Secret Service agents typically feel more comfortable if they can get the subject admitted to a hospital for observation and evaluation, and/or for treatment. Most prefer a voluntary admission route, in which the subject enters of his or her own volition. This management device becomes especially attractive when a protected person is about to visit the subject's area of residence and the subject is acting in a bizarre or irrational manner and has expressed a high degree of interest in that protected person.

---

*See presentation by R. K. Gable, page 169.

Management problems occur in instances in which a subject does not wish to be admitted for evaluation or treatment, and where he or she does not satisfy the criteria for involuntary commitment in the opinion of the admitting physician or the court. For this reason the Service usually tries to develop a working relationship with one or more sympathetic institutions and mental health professionals in each field office jurisdiction. Whatever the ethical dilemmas posed by this fact, clinicians pointed out that from a practical standpoint, Secret Service management problems are not solved by gaining the subject's admission to a hospital for observation and/or treatment. If the subject has voluntarily admitted himself to a hospital, he is free to leave at any time (although most states permit a delay in his release for a brief period if there is concern about his being dangerous). Because most hospitals have limited capacity for secure confinement, there is also the possibility that the patient will leave without authorization. Furthermore, overcrowding in mental hospitals, the trend toward deinstitutionalization of chronic mental patients, and liability issues often make admitting physicians reluctant to take on new potentially violent patients. In private hospitals, the subject's ability to pay the hospital charges or his access to third party reimbursement would also be a factor. These problems prompted some conferees to suggest that surveillance or other more intensive forms of street monitoring of such subjects might be more feasible, more reasonable, and more in keeping with the values of American society.

The presentation by Joseph English illustrated many of the dilemmas that the needs and mandate of the Secret Service may pose to admitting physicians and their hospitals. On the one hand, some physicians may wish to oblige the Service by admitting for involuntary observation and/or treatment a subject the Service considers dangerous. However, the subject may not meet the criteria for admission in that particular state. In the state of New York, for example, where Joseph English is director of psychiatry for St. Vincent's Hospital in Manhattan, it must be shown that the person (a) has a mental illness and can benefit from treatment, and (b) that he is "imminently dangerous" to himself or others to justify an emergency involuntary admission to the psychiatric service.

Secret Service Interventions and Deterrence

The Secret Service at present has no way to test the effectiveness of its interventions with subjects, in part because numerically there are so few assassination attempts on the lives of those it protects, and in part because it cannot afford to take the risk of not intervening where it thinks it should. Many conferees felt that the very existence of the Secret Service, and publicity about its activities, probably deters some persons who might otherwise be willing to risk an assassination attempt. Marvin Wolfgang, for instance, suggested that, because rational persons base their actions on their own perceptions as to the probability that they will be arrested, convicted, and/or imprisoned, the best overall strategy for the Secret Service is to cultivate the mystique of its own ubiquity. A highly visible and well-publicized Secret Service presence, he said, would probably be more effective as a deterrent than specific interventions undertaken with individual subjects. As far as Secret Service subjects are concerned, some conferees pointed out that the mere fact that a subject is under investigation--has been interviewed by the Secret Service, knows that he is under the Service's watchful eye, and is aware that his relatives or others familiar with him are being contacted about his activities and whereabouts--probably acts as a deterrent. On the other hand, Alfred Blumstein cautioned against assuming that a mentally disturbed individual responds to implicit or overt sanctions in the same way others might--especially if he does not value his own life.

Publicity about the activities and mission of the Secret Service, and its potential intervention, were regarded by conferees as legitimate and important forms of deterrence. A possible experiment to test the effectiveness of increased publicity about the Secret Service and its activities in reducing the number of threats and threateners was suggested.*

Specific Case Management Suggestions

1. For subjects who are not deemed committable, but are still in need of some sort of mental health intervention, R.K. Gable suggested referral to outpatient or private treatment by highly qualified mental health professionals. Therapy could consist of rerouting or eliminating the subject's direction of interest toward protected persons, by means of such behavior modification techniques as stimulus narrowing, systematic desensitization, and instruction in the management of anger.**

2. In Charles Halpern's opinion, much more attention should be devoted to developing management strategies for subjects who are not mentally ill--a small but consequential proportion of the current caseload of dangerous subjects.

---

*See Promising Research Opportunities: Some Specific Suggestions, page 77.

**See Gable's memorandum, page 171.

3. More active or frequent monitoring of dangerous subjects not presently confined might be in order. Such subjects are obviously more likely to present an imminent danger than equally hostile subjects who are confined to a mental or penal institution. Some conferees suggested that non-confined subjects, who typically constitute about half the caseload of dangerous subjects, might be monitored on a monthly rather than a three-month basis.

4. Conferees generally felt it would be useful for the Service to stratify and rank order the various management options it has, by level of intensity, intrusiveness, and potential severity of the consequences to the subject. For example, involuntary commitment to a mental or penal institution for threats or other behavior considered dangerous to a protected person would head the list in terms of severity of consequences for the subject. Voluntary admission to a mental hospital for observation would be a less severe management technique, but more intrusive than referring the subject for outpatient treatment, which in turn would be more intrusive than having a family member watch the subject.

Conferees also strongly urged the Secret Service to develop criteria to be used in deciding when to use each intervention strategy.

5. Several conferees suggested that the Secret Service experiment with greater use of the telephone to replace or supplement the personal interview for follow-up purposes, especially in view of the escalating cost of travel from field offices to the homes of subjects. The possibility that as much, if not more, information about the status of a subject could be gained by means of frequent telephone contact should be seriously entertained and investigated. Elissa Benedek, however, was opposed to the substitution of telephone interviewing for face-to-face contact with a subject for evaluation purposes. Interviewing in the home is a valuable source of cues that cannot be obtained by telephone, she felt. The telephone is, in her opinion, appropriate for use with collateral sources of information. Postcards and other notification devices also were suggested as potentially useful methods of letting a subject know the Secret Service is still interested in him.

6. Instead of attempting to commit a dangerous subject to a mental hospital for observation during the visit of a protected person to the subject's area of residence, it might be both simpler and more beneficial to the subject to suggest that he or she take a short "vacation" during the time-limited exposure of the protected person. Saleem Shah, however, cautioned the Service to be careful not to unwittingly provide positive reinforcement that could encourage problem subjects to return to the Service for more benign interventions.

7. For mentally or emotionally disturbed subjects, the provision of out-patient psychotherapy might be a beneficial intervention, which would not infringe on subjects' civil liberties.*

8. Some conferees questioned the value of reinterviewing dangerous subjects at all, as part of the quarterly investigation process. Although it is important to know a subject's whereabouts, there are ways to obtain such information without interviewing the subject. Only if a protected person travels to the subject's area of residence would an interview be desirable.

9. In connection with managing mentally ill or emotionally disburbed subjects, Shah suggested that agents be able to utilize mental health crisis centers, which would be open on a 24-hour basis.

10. Robert Fein suggested that the Secret Service experiment with interviewing dangerous subjects in locations other than their homes. For instance, conducting the interviews in Secret Service field offices might be less stressful for the agents involved, and thus more productive in terms of information yielded. (The primary advantage of interviewing subjects in their homes is that agents are able to gather clues from observation of the subject's surroundings.)

11. R. K. Gable suggested that the release of subjects from hospitals be made conditional upon some follow-up activities that would assist the Service in monitoring them, such as travel restrictions, medication compliance (if medication was prescribed upon discharge), periodic notification of the Secret Service or the hospital as to their whereabouts, and so forth. The use of case managers for this purpose was suggested.**

12. The institution of a computer-assisted system for making decisions about when to monitor and how to manage dangerous subjects was suggested by more than one conferee, and is discussed in the paper by Frazier and colleagues. Such a system would be programmed to include all relevant information collected on each subject, would be periodically updated to reflect current status, and would indicate occasions or time periods when individual subjects should be reassessed or monitored more closely, in terms of their own individual psychology and behavioral cycles (and their possible interaction with external events). Such a system could enable monitoring of each subject at intervals uniquely appropriate to him or her, and not necessarily on a quarterly basis.

---

*See paper by Michels, page 107.

**See Gable's memorandum, page 171, for elaboration of this point.

13. Marguerite Warren suggested that special agents be matched to subjects in ways that would facilitate Secret Service management goals. Not every agent, she suggested, is ideally suited to work with every subject.

### Ethical Implications of Case Management Practices

Conferees and Secret Service representatives alike expressed concerns about the ethical implications of current and proposed intervention strategies and management techniques for dangerous subjects. Several conferees thought the mere fact of being on QI might be a stigma for subjects, let alone the possible psychological damage and legal implications that could be associated with the various intervention strategies themselves.

One dilemma raised by Secret Service representatives concerned whether contacting a subject's employer for monitoring purposes constitutes an infringement of privacy and an unwarranted intrusion with potential for great harm. The pros and cons of using relatives and friends to gain information about a subject's attitudes and whereabouts were also discussed. The question of whether the Secret Service ever uses informants and undercover agents for intelligence gathering activities on subjects was also raised. Secret Service representatives explained that covert investigative activities are rarely employed, but such techniques do have some advantages. They may, for instance, enable the Service to gain a more accurate reading on the attitudes and activities of an occasional subject it believes is not being truthful with them, while not stigmatizing the subject with overtly intrusive types of interventions. Secret Service consultant Lewis Goldberg said he would regard the use of covert intelligence gathering activities on subjects as reprehensible in a free society. These and other such dilemmas were not resolved during the conference.*

### Recurrent and Persistent Case Management Problems

Conferees noted several circumstances that are likely to present intractable case management problems for the Secret Service. One, discussed earlier, is the easy availability of weapons in the United States. The problem of armed, irrational, and extremely disturbed persons was amply illustrated in one of the Secret Service case presentations, in which a subject discharged from a mental

---

*See also Legal and Ethical Aspects of Investigative Activities and Interventions, page 68.

hospital (and supposedly en route to admit himself to another mental hospital) was able to procure a weapon with which he soon killed a Secret Service agent.

A second problem, also noted earlier, is the trend toward deinstitutionalization of chronic mental patients, for whom there is at present virtually no organized aftercare.* This trend, in the opinion of those familiar with the problem, is likely to result in an increase in the Secret Service caseload, as well as an increase in subjects who are repeat or "recidivistic" threateners.

A third problem, illustrated in another case presentation, concerns the dependency that may be created if the Secret Service becomes for some subjects "the best friend they've ever had," in the words of one representative. For persons with chronic or recurring mental problems, repeated threats may gain the attention of the Secret Service and the gratification that the subject is seeking. Ironically, such dependency is particularly likely to occur to the extent that Secret Service interventions are benign rather than intrusive, and offered by way of sympathetic help. While there is a deterrent purpose in maintaining supportive contact with a subject, and attempting to neutralize, redirect, or refocus his or her direction of interest away from the protected persons, such supportive contact may, for some subjects, develop a level of attachment to the Service that will result in the subjects' provoking repeated monitoring contact. This constitutes a drain on resources of the Secret Service and is a problem not easily resolved, even if the Service utilizes mental health consultants.


LEGAL AND ETHICAL ASPECTS OF INVESTIGATIVE ACTIVITIES
AND INTERVENTIONS


Conferees' observations and suggestions with respect to the legal and ethical aspects of Secret Service information gathering activities and interventions with potentially dangerous subjects are summarized below.**

---

*See discussion of this problem under Relationship between the Secret Service and the Mental Health Community, page 49.

**See also Relationship between the Secret Service and the Mental Health Community.

## Balancing of Competing Values

The Secret Service mandate to protect the lives of highly placed leaders inevitably involves it in conflict with constitutionally-protected rights of individual citizens. The Service is thus perennially faced with having to maintain a delicate balance between its own mission and the civil liberties of those whom it investigates and monitors. Virtually all its activities in assessing and managing behavior potentially dangerous to protected persons involve legal and ethical dilemmas, and run the risk of involving the Service in costly litigation. Conferees were sympathetic to these concerns and suggested some ways to begin clarifying and resolving them.

## Availability of Legal Advice for Special Agents

Conferees advised that special agents assigned to intelligence gathering and monitoring duties should be thoroughly conversant with federal, state, and local statutes pertinent to their work. It is especially important, in the opinion of conferees, that agents be able to obtain expert legal advice at any time during the day or night in the handling of difficult cases. (Secret Service representatives assured conferees that such advice is indeed available to agents on a round-the-clock basis.) Conferees also suggested that the Service solicit legal advice and review in connection with (1) questionnaire construction and the wording of specific questions to be used with subjects, (2) the use to which information gathered from and about subjects is to be put, and (3) intervention strategies that might raise legal problems.

## Use of Least Restrictive Alternatives

As previously noted, the rule of thumb to be applied when intervening with subjects considered dangerous to protected persons should be to use the least restrictive alternatives commensurate with the need to protect. Application of this principle might mean, for instance, seeking outpatient evaluation and treatment rather than voluntary or involuntary commitment to a mental hospital for a subject who has a mental disorder but who poses uncertain or little imminent danger to a protected person.

In Charles Whitebread's opinion, it is especially important "to be sensitive to the civil liberties implications of the management of people labeled dangerous but whose conduct has not yet run afoul of the standards for the imposition of criminal sanction." Charles Halpern expressed similar concerns in noting that a significant number of Secret Service subjects have been neither formally diagnosed as mentally ill nor convicted of any crime. He argued in general for "humility in intervention."* In Halpern's view, conferees did not sufficiently explore possibilities for less coercive and less intrusive intervention measures.

On an optimistic note, Whitebread observed, "It is remarkable to me the number of thorny legal issues which have effectively been undercut or entirely eliminated by scientific innovation." In his view, technological solutions analogous to the use of metal detectors in airports might be developed to greatly enhance the safety of public leaders and minimally intrude upon individual civil liberties.

## A Standard of "Reasonableness"

Legal experts maintained that from a judicial standpoint, Secret Service information gathering and interventions are likely to be evaluated and judged in terms of their "reasonableness" and the degree to which procedures and criteria used in making decisions about individual subjects are applied in standardized and uniform ways, rather than in an arbitrary or capricious fashion. A program in which the least intrusive intervention measures commensurate with the need to protect government leaders have been consistently used should be judged reasonable. Likewise, a coherent "rationalized" program, in which the various management options have been fully elaborated and the bases for selecting particular alternatives for each case have been spelled out, should stand up in court.

To assess the impact of its own interventions on subjects, Judge Wald suggested that the Secret Service might take a retrospective look into its records to see whether any of its management activities have had serious legal ramifications, or "legally cognizable negative effects," on the subject(s) involved. If so, such intervention strategies should probably be modified or discontinued.

## Clarification of Legal and Ethical Issues

Several conferees and Secret Service representatives cited examples of situations that pose management dilemmas for special agents. For instance, there are subjects who have made no overt threats and who are not in violation of any law, but whom the Secret Service considers dangerous because of their high level of hostile interest in protected persons. As Loren Roth noted, such subjects

---

*Presentations by attorneys Whitebread and Halpern, pages 167 and 159, respectively, are relevant here.

may regard surveillance by the Service as an unwarranted intrusion into their privacy. The same dilemma might arise if the Secret Service conducted a "massive screening of all the politically sensitive groups," in Roth's words. Walter Menninger reiterated the Service's concern as to whether it is appropriate to contact a subject's employer as a management technique. Secret Service representatives acknowledged the dilemmas posed by such situations, which are common.

In view of the sensitivity of the legal and ethical dilemmas posed on a daily basis by many aspects of assessing and managing potentially dangerous subjects, several conferees recommended that the Secret Service seek clarification of several legal and ethical issues prior to adopting new policies or procedures. Included here would be confidentiality, privacy, free speech issues, and the myriad of federal and state laws and regulations concerning hospital commitment and other mental health issues.*

## IMPROVING AGENCY OPERATIONS: RESOURCE ALLOCATION AND MANAGEMENT ISSUES

Conferees quickly discovered that to be of genuine assistance to the Secret Service, they needed to be better informed about its mission and functions, and about its policies, procedures, capabilities, and deployment of resources (both monetary and staff). They felt that uninformed suggestions would be useless at best, and could even be harmful.

Secret Service representatives emphasized that the Service is primarily action-oriented and that staff members do not spend much time evaluating how well they are doing and analyzing how they might improve their operations. Resources are distributed among tasks largely on the basis of tradition, and standard operating procedures are often based on historical precedent. Conferees were impressed with the wealth of data that is on file and potentially available for analysis, but how little has been done with it to discover more efficient and effective ways of doing things.

To gain some understanding of Secret Service operations, conferees asked Secret Service representatives many questions about the allocation of time and other resources to various tasks, the

---

*See presentations by Michels and Gable, pages 163 and 169, respectively, and paper by Michels, page 107.

rationale for various procedures, and many aspects of the caseload of dangerous and not dangerous subjects. For instance, some conferees wanted to know how man-hours are allocated between threat assessment and direct protection. Others were curious as to whether the size of the dangerous caseload is "management-driven" or "dangerousness-driven," in Robert Michels' words. Loren Roth and others, as noted earlier, wanted to know why subjects must be judged to be either dangerous or not dangerous, a dichotomy felt to be both arbitrary and irrelevant. Alfred Blumstein and Frank Ochberg wanted to know how a budget cut or increase would affect the operations of the Intelligence Division. If the budget were doubled, would the Service double its caseload of dangerous subjects from 300 to 600, or would it monitor the present 300 more intensively? If the budget were halved, would the Division continue to monitor 300 dangerous subjects less thoroughly, or cut the load in half?

From what they were able to learn in the short time available, conferees suggested that the Service devote some consideration to the following topics:

### Characteristics of Cases and Caseload: Dangerous and Not Dangerous Subjects

Because of its action orientation, the Service has devoted relatively little time and financial resources to analyzing its case files of dangerous and never dangerous subjects. The Secret Service does not have at its fingertips, and cannot now easily retrieve, for instance, fundamental descriptive data about all cases and about various categories of cases: their socioeconomic and demographic characteristics, frequency of threat activity, mental status, and so forth. Neither does it have readily available information about average length of stay on quarterly investigation for dangerous subjects, reintroduction rates, frequency and intensity of monitoring, and other caseload characteristics. Conferees felt it essential that the Service begin to track such information in order to gain a better understanding of the validity of its own view of dangerousness and to facilitate research on the usefulness of the data it collects and its various assessment and monitoring activities.

### Case Referral System and Intake Process

As mentioned earlier, many conferees questioned the comprehensiveness of the case referral network and the administrative efficiency with which cases are referred to the Secret Service from government agencies and other sources. In general, conferees felt the Service should devote more time to case finding than it presently does. They were not convinced that incoming referrals represent the full range of persons or groups that might be dangerous to protected persons. Such referrals, they suggested, are probably too heavily biased toward the mentally disturbed, some of whom may be less lethal than persons who are not mentally ill. Further, they consist mainly of "announced" threateners--persons who have had, in the opinion of some conferees, the poor judgment to have disclosed their hostility beforehand. In contrast, persons or groups capable of planning and carefully plotting an attack, and having the good sense to keep their intentions to themselves, might be able to evade the referral network. Conferees suggested, therefore, that the Service assume a more active role in identifying sources of danger it might have overlooked, and redirect some of its funds accordingly.

Conferees also noted the opportunity for slippage in the inter-agency communication and referral process--a possible source of serious error--and suggested the Service re-evaluate its inter-agency communication system.

Several conferees--most notably Robert Michels--suggested that the intake process, by which incoming cases are screened prior to deployment for investigation, should be re-evaluated. It was Michels' opinion that cases may have to be screened more carefully in order to prevent the system from being clogged with an extraordinarily high number of false positives. Michels suggested that a new short form assessment protocol be developed to screen for relevance prior to a full blown investigation of each referral (which current procedures require). Local consultants with appropriate expertise might be used to screen incoming cases.

Operations Research: Development of a Management Information System

Fundamental to any improvement in Secret Service operations is the development of an adequate management information system, which would make research on agency operations possible.* Conferees were unanimously agreed that the voluminous data on file about individual subjects, as well as the wealth of experience accumulated by seasoned agents, should be systematically extracted and computerized for research and analytic purposes. Such data, if made available in readily usable form, should help the Service critically examine its own operations and procedures, and ultimately gain a better understanding of the validity of its activities.

---

*The present management information system is used primarily to identify threateners and to locate subjects for advance work prior to the arrival of protected person to their areas of residence.

The Legislative Mandate:   Some Problems

Saleem Shah questioned the rationale behind the list of persons Congress has mandated the Secret Service to protect. In his opinion, Secret Service resources that might profitably be used elsewhere are distracted by the duty to protect persons who are neither in the public eye nor in any particular danger as to their safety. Secret Service representatives acknowledged that the need to protect persons who face no greater risk than that of the ordinary citizen consigns some agents to duties they find boring and irrelevant. Alternative strategies for expressing concern for the welfare of such individuals are discussed by Shah in his paper.

GUIDELINES FOR ESTABLISHING A RESEARCH AND CONSULTATION CAPACITY IN THE BEHAVIORAL SCIENCES AND CLINICAL DISCIPLINES

In both plenary and small group sessions, conferees devoted considerable attention to the question, "How can the Secret Service become a more informed consumer of behavioral research?," initially posed by the Secret Service to the planning committee preparing for this conference. There was unanimous agreement, among conferees and Secret Service representatives alike, that the Intelligence Division should develop a research and consultation capacity in the behavioral sciences and clinical disciplines relevant to its mission.

At present, the Division has neither the staff capability to carry out its own research, nor the capacity to evaluate incoming research proposals. It has only one staff member with research listed among his many other duties. The Service has contracted for behavioral research in the past, but its experiences with contractors have often been less than satisfactory, in part because it has lacked the internal capacity to define and evaluate desired research products. As pointed out by Don Gottfredson, Saleem Shah, and others, unless the Intelligence Division builds some research capability into its operations, it will be unable to use its very considerable wealth of information on file and the experiences and expertise of its special agents, to learn what works and what doesn't work and to improve its own operations. It was the opinion of all present that now is the time for such reflection, analysis, and evaluation to begin.

Developing a Research Capability

Although there was agreement on the need for the Service to develop a behavioral science research capacity, conferees differed somewhat as to the ways in which a quality research program should be achieved. Much of their disagreement was about the most appropriate locus for such capacity-building to begin. As Robert Michels noted, the best science in the shortrun will be done outside the Service by contract, but the greatest impact on Secret Service operations will come from the development of a staff research capability. Several conferees, most notably Alfred Blumstein, argued that the first step in building such a research capacity should be to establish a research advisory board, external to the Service, which would oversee its development. In his opinion, it would be next to impossible at present for the Secret Service, a small federal agency, to attract as employees persons with the level of research competence and skill that would best serve its needs. Until it became sizable, any research unit established within the Service would be of low quality, according to Blumstein. Brian Jenkins, like Blumstein, also saw advantages in the creation of an ad hoc research advisory group. He proposed that such a group use the suggestions of this report as a starting point and assist the Service in (1) determining the nature, size, and direction of a possible behavioral science research program; (2) deciding what proportion of the research effort should be handled by staff and what proportion extramurally through contracts or grants; (3) determining staffing needs and staff composition; and (4) defining the nature of any long- and short-term contractual agreements the Service might enter into.

In contrast, Billings, English, Gottfredson, and Shah all argued for development of a staff research capacity from the start. Billings pointed out that for an advisory group to have a sufficient influence on an agency, there must be "educated consumers within-house." Shah said that an agency that has operating responsibilities cannot afford to delegate to outsiders research related to the exercise of those responsibilities. In Shah's opinion, therefore, the Secret Service must from the start have at least the nucleus of its own research staff, to be further developed over time. If an outside advisory group were created, a research staff would be needed in order to put its recommendations into practice and to provide a link to senior management personnel. The functions of a research staff would also include deciding what research suggestions of the advisory group are worth pursuing, evaluating proposals, and translating research results and findings into operationally useful information.

These two viewpoints were fairly readily combined in a consensus that both staff and advisory research initiatives should be undertaken simultaneously. An advisory group, working with a skeleton research staff would probably best suit the needs of the Service at present. The research advisory group might have some or all of these characteristics and functions:

● it would consist of a panel of behavioral science experts drawn from several different disciplines, similar to but smaller than the panel of scientists, scholars and clinicians assembled for this conference

● its members might spend some time on site at Secret Service headquarters or field offices familiarizing themselves with Service policies and procedures, so that their suggestions would be practically relevant to ongoing activities

● it would be an ad hoc organization, in existence only on an interim basis, until such time as the Secret Service itself was prepared to take over its functions

● its main goals would be to assist the Secret Service in developing its own capacity to define its research needs, gaining entree to the behavioral science research community, exploring relationships with other federal agencies conducting relevant research, beginning to develop a coherent research program, procuring and evaluating behavioral science research, and developing its own research staff

● it could provide direction to the Service in implementing some suggestions of conferees, such as developing a management information system useful for evaluating the effectiveness of its own activities and operations, descriptively analyzing and profiling its dangerous and not dangerous subjects, and commissioning specific research studies

● it could stimulate research by behavioral scientists in the academic and private sectors on issues of concern to the Secret Service.

Use of Behavioral Science and Clinical Consultants

Conferees were unanimously agreed that the use of behavioral science and clinical experts as regular consultants should be encouraged as a means of obtaining advice in areas of specific need. They noted that the Service would always value a working relationship with individual consultants of its own choosing. Most conferees thought the Service was in a good position to exercise its own judgment as to the usefulness of particular consultants. Roth again cautioned, however, that for consultation to be truly useful, the consultants may need to immerse themselves in the day-to-day activities of the Service--to see how decisions are made, how interviews are conducted, how cases are referred for investigation, and so forth. Speaking for himself, Roth said that after such immersion he might "be in a better position to understand the relevancy of what I know to . . . what they have to do." Without such detailed understanding of how the Secret Service operates, he felt, consultants might make "deadly blunders" in their naivete.

## PROMISING RESEARCH OPPORTUNITIES: SPECIFIC SUGGESTIONS

Numerous ideas and suggestions for research projects were offered during the conference. Many of these are discussed under other headings of this report. Some conference presentations, papers, and memoranda also discuss specific research proposals. The following is a synopsis of suggestions that emerged during plenary and workshop sessions, and that are not fully discussed elsewhere in this report.

Conferees were emphatic that research and experiments to test the validity and usefulness of Intelligence Division activities are indispensable for improving the effectiveness and efficiency of the Division's operations. Although research may be viewed as a luxury which an operating agency can ill afford, without it there can be no genuine progress in understanding and fully "rationalizing" decision-making processes, procedures, and policies. In the words of Saleem Shah, the mere accumulation of experience without appropriate feedback and research is like "throwing darts at a dart board . . . in a darkened room."*

### High Priority Research-Related Tasks

Conferees were in near unanimous agreement that three tasks to facilitate future research should be undertaken promptly: a retrospective descriptive analysis of file data on dangerous (and, if time permits, never dangerous) subjects; development of behavioral indices and scales to measure more precisely the level of danger posed by subject behaviors; and the creation of a management information system aimed at systematically improving operations. The accomplishment of these tasks should provide the Intelligence Division with a rudimentary capacity and data base of information for testing hypotheses and conducting studies it might wish to undertake in the future.

---

*The importance and usefulness of experimental studies, and some possible Secret Service applications, are discussed by Lincoln Moses in his paper, page 113. A member of the planning committee, Dr. Moses was unable to attend the conference.

Descriptive Analysis of Subject Files

Conferees felt hampered in their efforts to provide useful advice by the lack of descriptive information about Secret Service subjects as a group and various segments of the dangerous and never dangerous caseload--their socioeconomic, demographic, and psychological and personality characteristics; mental status and history; criminal history; types and frequency of threat activity or other dangerous behavior, and so forth.

With the exception of Hillel Einhorn and Kenneth Hammond (for reasons discussed below), all conferees agreed that as its first and highest research priority the Intelligence Division should develop a descriptive summary of the characteristics of its dangerous subjects (and also its never dangerous subjects, if time permits). In order to do this, variables or data items of interest must be specified, extracted from the file data on each case (or a sample of cases), processed for computer use, and analyzed. Analysis of such descriptive data, for instance, might yield a better understanding of what factors--at least in the minds of Secret Service special agents--differentiate dangerous from never dangerous subjects, and assist the Service in evaluating the validity of agent decisions. In any case, availability of relevant data about subjects in computerized form could provide a starting point for empirical research to test a variety of hypotheses.

Einhorn and Hammond were not optimistic that retrospective analysis of file data would be a productive undertaking. The very fact that the Secret Service has intervened in the lives of its subjects influences their subsequent behaviors, in many cases probably changing the outcomes or behaviors that might have been observed had no such interventions taken place. This problem of treatment effects would invalidate any study of agent decision-making that compared outcomes or subsequent behaviors of subjects classified as dangerous and never dangerous.

Measurement Improvement

Many conferees felt that to facilitate research and evaluation of agent predictions, revised assessment and management instruments should contain many scaled items, which would enable a subject's behaviors and activities to be rated in terms of their potential danger to protected persons. For instance, a scale of undesirable events, or threshold behaviors, short of an attempted assassination--a very rare event--might be developed for this purpose. Such undesirable and potentially dangerous behaviors might include appearing in proximity to a protected person with a weapon, or plotting the movements of a protected person on maps from one's home.*

## Expanding the Management Information System to Support Operations Research

The Intelligence Division uses its present management information system primarily to assist in the identification of threats and threateners, and to locate subjects during advance work prior to visits of protected persons to their areas of residence. The system is not now designed for research in support of modifying and improving operating procedures. Many conferees felt that the Service could benefit from the development of a management information system programmed for retrieval of such items as the rate at which cases are added to and deleted from the system, the average length of time or number of quarters a subject is consecutively classified as dangerous, the rate at which closed (not presently dangerous) cases are re-opened (newly classified as dangerous) for investigation, the amount of agent time spent in different aspects of assessing and managing subjects, and so forth. Analysis of such data on a periodic basis would aid the Service in discovering which of its operations are too time-consuming or inefficient in terms of the benefits yielded, and other matters pertinent to the effective and efficient operation of the Division.

## Other Research Suggested

### Testing Alternative Management Methods

Several conferees pointed out opportunities for experiments that could be developed to test the feasibility and usefulness of different assessment or management strategies and procedures. Such experiments might be conducted by giving half the experimental cases one treatment, the other half another treatment, and then later comparing the groups on the basis of pre-designated outcome measures. Examples of such experiments include testing the effectiveness and efficiency of

● telephone contact compared with personal interviewing for follow-up investigations of "dangerous" subjects

● quarterly investigation and monthly investigation of "dangerous" subjects

---

*See Assessing Potentially Dangerous Behavior, page 24.

● field office interviewing and at-home interviewing of subjects

● male-female teams of interviewers and male-only interviewing teams (tested separately with male and female subjects).

Conferees attached one proviso to all such experiments:  there must be no diminution in the present level or intensity of subject monitoring, in view of the unacceptability of an untoward event, such as an assassination attempt.  That is, the Service cannot afford to experimentally decrease or eliminate its monitoring activities, but can only vary in the way such monitoring activities might be carried out.

## Testing the Deterrent Effects of Publicity

Although the Service cannot afford the risk of not intervening with subjects it considers dangerous, there may be other, indirect, ways to test the capacity of the Secret Service to deter behavior potentially dangerous to those it protects.  One suggestion was to compare the volume of threats in a city where local Secret Service activities are highly publicized in the news media with the level of threat activity in a comparable (matched) city where the Service's activities are less well publicized.

## Prospective Studies Using Revised Data Collection Instruments

Even though some conferees were skeptical about retrospective analyses of existing file data, there was a broad consensus that valid prospective experimental studies could be designed for use with new subjects, once the data collection instruments were revised and fully computerized.*

## Studies of Agent Decision-Making

At present, agent decision-making with respect to the determination of dangerousness is intuitive and not very well understood either by the agents making those decisions or by their supervisors.  Many conferees thought that more attention should be devoted to determining how agents actually reach their decisions. (One study on agent decision-making is in progress, as noted earlier.)  The various agent decision-making patterns that emerge should be explicitly described and evaluated, and, if relevant, the better patterns used for training purposes.

---

*See Assessing Potentially Dangerous Behavior, page 24, for a discussion of proposed instrument revisions.

Inter-agent reliability studies would also be helpful, in the opinion of several conferees. That is, once the criteria for decision-making with respect to dangerousness have been made explicit, agents could be compared in terms of their ability to reach appropriate decisions based on the criteria specified. Agents found to be less reliable than others in the quality of their decision-making could receive additional training or be reassigned to other duties.

Testing the Effectiveness of the System

Because the Secret Service has limited experience with actual assassination, it does not have secure knowledge that its information gathering activities, interventions with subjects, and protective measures are effective in preventing or deterring attempts on the lives of those it protects. Further, an adverse event--whether an attempted or successful assassination--creates severe morale problems for Secret Service employees, whether or not the Service can in any way be faulted for neglect of duty. Clinicians pointed out that Secret Service agents contemplating a possible assassination are in a situation analogous to psychiatrists facing the possibility that one of their patients may commit suicide (also an infrequent but highly perturbing act). Clinicians and behavioral scientists encouraged the Secret Service to confront squarely their fear of negligence, retrospectively analyze failures, and to anticipate and prepare for possible errors through a variety of research and training activities.

The first two suggestions below are for scenario construction studies with training implications, proposed by Hillel Einhorn as ways for Secret Service employees to critically examine their operations and detect potential flaws or loopholes in their information gathering, subject management, and protective activities against assassination.

Fault-tree analysis is a method of examining how large systems break down. Every conceivable scenario by which a protected person could be assassinated would be run through the Secret Service defensive-protective system to determine whether any routes to assassination are potentially available.

Simulating an assassination assumes a rational-actor model of behavior--that a person will act rationally and logically to pursue his goal, however crazy or ill-advised that goal might seem. For instance, such a rational actor might start with the notion or delusion that the president of the United States is a tool of creatures from outer space and must therefore be forcibly removed from office and killed. Given this information, the agents' task

81

would be to determine how such a person might go about trying to assassinate the president. The various possibilities would be rehearsed in order to detect the system's weak spots, which might permit him to succeed.

Other suggested studies include a test of the adequacy of the inter-agency case referral system, employing fabricated letters or actors to find out whether cases are regularly and consistently referred to the Secret Service (for instance, from the White House mail room or various government agencies) in accordance with guidelines issued.

## CAREER PATTERNS AND SELECTION OF SPECIAL AGENTS

### Career Patterns

The Service's present policy is that recruits should be generalists for the first six years of their Service careers, rotating through several tours of duty and learning something about many different functions, but not becoming an expert in any of them. Many conferees, especially the clinicians, wondered about the wisdom and advisability of the Secret Service's preference for generalists over specialists among its special agents.* The Service's position derives in part from the belief that knowledge and experience gained in each rotation contributes to overall agent effectiveness, and will be a valuable asset in future assignments. While this view may be rooted in habit and tradition, rather than in a detailed and current examination of needs, the Service has a pragmatic reason for favoring generalists over specialists: in many of the smaller field offices to which special agents will be assigned during their careers, the entire Secret Service operation is not big enough to warrant specialists in different kinds of work. In accordance with the need for individuals who can perform a variety of Secret Service functions, the promotional opportunities for generalists are far better than they are for specialists throughout the Service. (As a rule, special agents advance within the Service by proving themselves to be good at everything.)

In response to questions from conferees, Secret Service representatives acknowledged that many special agents do not enjoy the interviewing and investigative work connected with assessing and managing potentially dangerous subjects. Some, for instance, find

---

*See also paper by Michels, page 107.

82

the interviewing distasteful or inherently stressful and/or the investigative work useless or boring. These agents often prefer other assignments, such as counterfeit detection, protective detail (physical protection), or the more conventional police types of work. Conferees were sympathetic to this problem--especially those whose experience with dangerous patients has made them familiar with the stress of dealing with potentially violent individuals over long periods of time. They also understood that having to generate apparently purposeless paperwork--in view of the infrequency of assassination attempts--can lead to discouragement and disillusionment.

On the other hand, Secret Service representatives noted that there are some agents who thrive on the kind of work involved in assessing and managing subjects, and seem to be skilled and talented at interviewing and other aspects of the job. Conferees wondered whether such agents might be identified early in their careers (or even selected for the Secret Service on the basis of their interest and capabilities in these areas), encouraged to develop their potential along these lines, and permitted to be specialists rather than generalists. In this connection, some conferees challenged the Service preference for generalists. Marguerite Warren, for instance, noted that her experience with juvenile offender programs has led her to conclude--and there is evidence in the literature to suggest--that some individuals are less suited to performing a wide variety of different and unrelated tasks. In her opinion, such persons should be permitted to develop their preferred skills or native abilities to the maximum, and be assigned only to those tasks which they do best and/or prefer. She contended that if there are agents who are particularly astute in diagnosing dangerousness on the basis of interviews with subjects, and others who are good at records investigation or case management tasks, the Service should consider splitting these functions traditionally handled by one agent (or two, acting as a team), thus permitting several agents to be involved in different aspects of the same case.

In keeping with the view that there may very well be a place for specialists in the field of assessing and managing potentially dangerous subjects, conferees felt that promotional opportunities and meaningful career ladders should be developed for recruits who demonstrate capability in these areas, noting that persons who are excellent candidates for such work might not survive the years of varied assignments required before an agent has the opportunity to select a few areas for concentration. Further, in Robert Fein's opinion, special efforts must be made to retain and reward agents who have already worked their way up the ladder and are particularly adept at interviewing or other assessment and management tasks; theirs is a valuable skill which should not be lost through inadvertent and/or unjustifiable Secret Service policy.

## Agent Recruitment and Selection

Many of the suggestions for improved functioning of the Secret Service Intelligence Division have implications for recruitment and selection of special agents who will work in the area of assessing and managing potentially dangerous subjects. Although agent recruitment and selection were aired less fully than other issues, conferees did have a few observations on these topics, which are discussed below.

### Broadening the Applicant Pool

Special agents at present are overwhelmingly white, middle class, and male. Although precise figures were not available, Secret Service representatives did indicate that the caseload of subjects with whom such agents typically come in contact includes both females and members of minority groups (especially blacks and hispanics). To facilitate communication between agents and subjects, who are likely to be of the opposite sex or of a different racial/ethnic background, conferees suggested that the Service make a concerted effort to recruit both women and minorities as special agents. While there is as yet no solid evidence that matching agents to subjects on the basis of sex and race/ethnicity would increase the relevance or validity of the information elicited for decision-making, experienced clinicians and behavioral science researchers have found that the sex and race/ethnicity of the parties involved in an interview often does make a difference.* Experiments to test whether matching by sex, race, and ethnicity affect the relevance or validity of the information elicited from subjects could, of course, be designed.

### Agent Selection: Desirable Incoming Qualifications and Skills

Whatever their subsequent career patterns (generalist or specialist), incoming special agents who at any time will be assessing or managing potentially dangerous subjects should possess some basic qualifications and skills at the time they join the Service.

Incoming special agents should be able to communicate clearly in English. Writing skills are especially important, as agents spend a great deal of time writing reports for use by others. Agents should also be able to observe and report accurately on what they see and hear during an interview with a subject, members of his family or employer, or anyone else who might be interviewed in connection with an initial or follow-up investigation.

---

*See Frazier's presentation and paper by Frazier and colleagues, pages 133 and 93, respectively.

Whether an incoming special agent should be a skilled interviewer upon entering the Secret Service will depend upon the career pattern he or she will follow--specialist or generalist. For agents who will specialize in assessing and managing potentially dangerous subjects, demonstrated interviewing skills probably should be among the incoming qualifications. Conferees generally supported Kenneth Hammond's contention that potential recruits are unlikely to differ substantially in their decision-making and prediction capabilities, and thus should not be selected on grounds of apparent superiority in these areas. As far as other skills and abilitites relevant to assessing and managing potentially dangerous subjects are concerned, Robert Michels said that it is easier to select persons who already demonstrate capabilities in some of these areas than to train those without them--especially such qualities as interpersonal sensitivity, empathy, and "psychological mindedness."*

## TRAINING OF SPECIAL AGENTS

### Desirable Skills and Substantive Competencies

#### Interviewing and Observation Skills

Unless they enter the Service with fundamental skills and experience in interviewing both normal and mentally disturbed persons, special agents must be trained in basic interviewing techniques and in special techniques to be used with mentally ill and potentially violent subjects. Similarly, agents must develop their powers of observation, use them to gain information about subjects, and report accurately on what they have observed.**

#### Ability to Detect Sources of Error in Judgment

Einhorn suggested, and others concurred, that special agents should be trained to recognize common sources of error or invalidity in judgment and decision-making, and to be on guard against them in their own work. (The Service has already begun to incorporate this topic into its training program.) For instance, they should understand that because assassination is a statistically rare event

---

*See paper by Michels, page 107.

**Presentations by Frazier and Menninger are relevant here (pages 133 and 147, respectively), as is the paper by Frazier and colleagues (page 93).

in the United States, most of the subjects they classify as "dangerous" who are also mentally ill and have a history of violence would not attempt to assassinate a protected person, even if left to their own devices.

## Knowledge of Statutory and Case Law

Judge Wald and other lawyers emphasized that agents must be thoroughly grounded in federal and state statutes and case law relevant to their work.

## Substantive Knowledge in the Area of Mental Health

Conferees agreed that special agents should receive more training in the area of mental health than they now do, because of the high proportion of dangerous cases in which mental or emotional disorder is apparently present.

Conferees discussed not only the positive contributions of a training program in mental health, but also its limitations--what it cannot and should not aspire to do. A mental health training program should not, for example, attempt to make psychiatrists out of special agents; nor should it overwhelm them with jargon and psychiatric nomenclature. Likewise, therapeutic and criminal justice goals and roles should be recognized as distinct from each other, and no attempt should be made to divert special agents from their foremost duty to function as law enforcement officials and guardians of the safety of protected persons. Many conferees considered the agents themselves to be the experts in judging dangerousness to protected persons, and thought they should not have their decisions unduly affected by the views of mental health professionals.

Conferees substantially agreed that special agents who assess and manage potentially dangerous subjects need more extensive and detailed training in psychopathology and in the use of clinical management techniques and options. Present training activities of most special agents in these areas are superficial and do not systematically expose agents to a wide range of mental and emotional disorders and a versatile repertoire of techniques appropriate for managing dangerous subjects.

Special agents rely too heavily on the mental health and criminal justice system for case disposition, in the opinion of some conferees. A mental health training program should include instruction in monitoring techniques and options which agents themselves can use, without resorting to the mental health or criminal justice systems. Agents also should understand the uses and effects of medications frequently prescribed for mentally or emotionally disturbed patients. They should be taught how patients/subjects released from mental hospitals on medication are or should be monitored for medication compliance, whether by mental health personnel or by Secret Service agents acting or assisting as case managers.*

## Developing Skills of Agents

### Role Play and Use of Videotape Recorders

The Secret Service Office of Training uses role play and videotape recorders for initial and follow-up training of special agents assigned to assessing and managing potentially dangerous subjects. Conferees considered these to be valuable instructional aids for teaching and refining interviewing techniques and for developing agents' self-confidence in interview settings. Both role playing and videotaping can improve performance by providing feedback under safe conditions (in contrast to the often stressful conditions under which actual interviews with subjects take place). Either method might help special agents learn how to ask appropriate follow-up questions to elicit relevant information not volunteered by a subject. Nevertheless, conferees also emphasized that there is no substitute for exposure to and experience with live cases during training. That is, experience with psychiatric patients and others (whether mentally disturbed or not) who are or resemble subjects potentially dangerous to those the Secret Service protects is an indispensable component of any such training program.**

### Internship in a Clinical Setting

In the opinion of several clinicians, an effective way to expose special agents to patients and at the same time familiarize them with a wide range of clinical disorders and mental health issues would be to establish special training programs for them in mental hospitals or other mental health facilities. A carefully supervised apprenticeship, clerkship, or internship in such a setting might be arranged on a two-day per week basis for two months or on a half-day basis for six weeks, or on a more intensive basis for special agents

---

*The content of training activities in the mental health field is also discussed below, under "Internship in a Clinical Setting."

**See paper by Michels, page 107.

who will devote a good part of their Secret Service careers to
assessing and managing potentially dangerous subjects. The goals of
such a program would be to

 • expose special agents to a broad cross-section of mentally
and emotionally disturbed persons

 • help them understand the differences between the
(potentially) violent and non-violent mentally ill

 • permit them to observe mental health professionals making
"imminent dangerousness" decisions

 • enable them to watch clinicians interview mentally and
emotionally disturbed patients and thereby sharpen their own
intuitive and interviewing skills

 • increase their repertoire of responses to and judgments
about mentally and emotionally disturbed subjects

 • expose them to a full range of clinical management
techniques and increase their understanding of the circumstances
appropriate to each

 • help them feel more at ease in dealing with mental health
professionals and institutions

 • enable them to handle their own stress more effectively when
dealing with disturbed subjects.*


Simulations, Gaming, and Senario Construction

      Frank Ochberg and others suggested simulation, gaming, and
scenario construction as devices useful for teaching special agents
how to recognize and deal with less familiar but apparently
increasing possibilities of harm to protected persons, such as
hostage taking extortion, and terrorism. Such techniques are
especially valuable in helping trainees anticipate and rehearse
possible future events, thus contributing to their overall
preparedness. R K. Gable and Hillel Einhorn, among others, noted
that these techniques can also be used to sharpen agents' abilities
to distinguish real from pseudo threats: true suicide notes from
fabrications, threat messages written by real subjects from phony
threat messages, the truly mentally ill from actors posing as
disturbed subjects, and so forth.

---

      *Also see papers by Frazier and colleagues and by Michels,
pages 93 and 107, respectively.

## Special Training Program for Senior Agents

Joseph English proposed a special training program for senior agents who are experienced and expert in assessing and managing potentially dangerous subjects. Such agents would be subsidized for post-graduate study in mental health, conducted by a teaching hospital in a hospital setting. Upon completion of this program, agents so trained would return to the Secret Service to instruct and supervise less experienced or beginning special agents in the mental health aspects of their preparation for assessing and managing potentially dangerous subjects. The principal advantage of such a program is that it would enable the Service to develop its own competency in the mental health field, which would lessen the need for Secret Service personnel to consult outsiders about subjects presenting mental and emotional problems. Elissa Benedek additionally noted that agents in training would also be more receptive and willing to ask questions if they received their instruction in this field from specially trained Secret Service agents rather than from mental health professionals.

## Training to Improve Agent Decision-Making

Although little is known about how agents reach their dangerousness decisions,* conferees and Secret Service representatives alike acknowledged that there are some agents who, by virtue of extensive experience and/or innate talent, are notably adept at making decisions appropriate to the circumstances--whether they do so by an intuitive or rational process. Conferees suggested that the decision-making processes of these agents be carefully analyzed and used to model the decision-making behaviors of less experienced, less gifted, and novice agents. In the short run, this activity would probably increase the reliability with which decisions are made--the extent to which all agents use the same criteria in making their decisions. It would also enable supervisors and training personnel to pinpoint agents whose decision-making skills need improvement and/or who should be reassigned to other duties because of inadequate performance in this area. In the long run, improving the reliability of agent decisions would probably make it easier to test whether agent decisions are correct in terms of the actual level of risk posed by subjects.

---

*A study of agent decision-making is currently in progress.

## Retraining and Corrective Feedback

In-service training for special agents is and should continue to be updated periodically, in order to sharpen skills and introduce new techniques and more sophisticated knowledge. Agents should be given feedback on their performance and taught to recognize their own errors and correct them. Untoward events, whether attempted or successful assassinations, killing or maiming of Secret Service agents, or close calls, should be reviewed with all special agents in an honest and non-defensive manner, so as to locate possible errors in judgment and inadequate protective measures. Such reviews constitute an important source of feedback on operations, as well as an appropriate mechanism by which government agencies and their employees assume responsibility for examining their own actions.

# NOTE

[1]Under Title 18 of the United States Code, section 3056 (18 USC 3056), the United States Secret Service is authorized to protect the following persons: the President of the United States and members of his immediate family; the President-elect and members of his immediate family, unless the members decline such protection; the Vice President or other officer next in order of succession to the Office of the President and members of his immediate family, unless the members decline such protection; the Vice President elect and members of his immediate family, unless the members decline such protection; a former President and his wife during his lifetime; the widow of a former President until her death or remarriage; the minor children of a former President until they reach age 16, unless such protection is declined; visiting heads of foreign states or foreign governments, and, at the direction of the President, other distinguished foreign visitors to the United States and official representatives of the United States performing special missions abroad; major Presidential and Vice Presidential candidates, unless such protection is declined; the spouse of a major Presidential or Vice Presidential nominee, commencing a maximum of 120 days prior to the general Presidential election.

The number of persons protected by the Secret Service on any given day averages around 25 to 30, but may be as high as 70.

The Secret Service also relies on Section 3056 as its basic legal authority to collect and disseminate intelligence information in connection with its protective duties. The Service is specifically authorized by section 3056 to detect and arrest any person who violates the so-called "threat statute" (18 USC 871). This statute states in part: "(a) Whoever knowingly and willfully deposits for conveyance in the mail or for a delivery from any post office or by any letter carrier any letter, paper, writing, print, missive, or document containing any threat to take the life of or to inflict bodily harm upon the President of the United States, the President-elect, the Vice President or other officer next in the order of succession to the office of the President of the United States, or the Vice President-elect, or knowingly or willfully otherwise makes any such threat against the President, President-elect, Vice President or other officer next in the order of succession to the office of President, or Vice President-elect, shall be fined not more than $1,000 or imprisoned not more than five years, or both."

# PROBLEMS IN ASSESSING AND MANAGING DANGEROUS BEHAVIOR

Shervert H. Frazier, M.D.*
Psychiatrist-in-Chief
McLean Hospital
Belmont, Massachusetts

McLean Hospital is a private non-profit psychiatric hospital affiliated with the Massachusetts General Hospital and is a teaching hospital of the Harvard Medical School. Founded in the 19th Century, the hospital is noted for providing evaluation and treatment for severely disturbed men and women, especially those who need secure and comprehensive inpatient care.

In 1975, the Massachusetts Department of Correction initiated an innovative contract with McLean Hospital under which McLean would be responsible for providing psychiatric and psychological expertise in the evaluation and treatment of male patients at the Massachusetts maximum security psychiatric facility, the Bridgewater State Hospital for the Criminally Insane. Since 1975, McLean clinicians have been evaluating and treating the most psychotic and violent men in Massachusetts. Currently, a staff of 16 McLean psychiatrists, psychologists, and social workers provide mental health services at Bridgewater. Recently the Department of Correction expanded the contract so that McLean clinicians now provide psychiatric services throughout the state correctional system.

The United States Secret Service (USSS) requested that the National Academy of Sciences convene a conference on the question of how behavioral research can aid the Secret Service to protect governmental leaders. As a result, a team of McLean/Bridgewater psychologists and psychiatrists considered these questions. The Secret Service seeks further knowledge to aid in its identification, assessment, and management of persons who might be dangerous to those it protects. Specifically, the USSS asks about objective indicators of "dangerousness," decision-making priorities for assessing an

---

*In collaboration with Park E. Dietz, M.D., M.P.H.; Ronald S. Ebert, Ph.D.; Sara Eddy, Ed.D.; Robert A. Fein, Ph.D.; William S. James, M.D.; Wesley E. Profit, Ph.D.; Renate C. Wack, Dipl. Psych., M.P.H., all of the McLean/Bridgewater Program, McLean Hospital, Belmont, Massachusetts.

individual's dangerousness, interviewing styles and strategies that are effective with individuals who threaten the protected, the relationship of "dangerousness" to social factors such as group affiliations, family, and local or national events, the management of individuals who are seen as dangerous, and improvement of relationships between the Secret Service and mental health and behavioral science professionals.

To consider these questions, we reviewed thoroughly a substantial literature on "dangerousness" and the few rare articles on assassins. We met with Secret Service agents from Washington and Boston. We evaluated our experience in assessing, managing, and treating men and women who assault and murder.

Although the literature on "dangerousness" is substantial, the concept of dangerousness is still not adequately defined. Because anyone can be dangerous, the Secret Service is concerned only with persons whose specific aim is to harm those it protects. It works to identify, assess, and manage the small particular subset of people who might act on thoughts or impulses they have about injuring or killing government leaders and/or their families. Secret Service agents in Boston report that increasing numbers of mentally disordered individuals threaten the president primarily to get attention and care. These people might or might not be dangerous to a protected person and often need sophisticated assessment by mental health professionals.

The demands on the Secret Service are growing.

"Deinstitutionalization" of large, antiquated state mental hospitals has sent thousands of mentally disordered men and women into the community. However laudable the goals of deinstitutionalization, it is clear that mental health services (and controls) for the mentally ill have changed dramatically. In Massachusetts, police, judges, and criminal justice agencies report that increasing numbers of mentally ill persons are arrested for crimes of all kinds, minor and major.

The identification, assessment, and management of individuals who threaten government leaders is a difficult and complex task. In this report, we present factors we consider in determining whether a person warrants detailed clinical evaluation for dangerousness. We describe the outline of a detailed assessment. We discuss the selection of Secret Service agents, the composition of agent corps and squads, the need for male-female interviewing teams, the support of agents, liaison with mental health and behavioral science professionals, and the collection, storage, and analysis of data relevant to the Secret Service's mission. We include a memorandum on potential female assassins and a set of recommendations.

I.    Identification of Potential Assassins

In our work with psychotic assailants and murderers of both the famous and the not-so-famous, we have identified some criteria we use when considering an individual's likelihood of future violent behavior.  We are aware that no valid, reliable, objective criteria exist which will definitively predict an individual's "dangerousness."  We have, however, identified several factors that could lead us to do a preliminary assessment of such an individual. We consider the following factors:

A.  History of mental illness
    1. Has he/she a history of acute psychosis, especially with paranoid symptoms?
    2. Has he/she a history of suicide attempts?
    3. Has he/she a history of delusional ideas in which there is has a sense of mission or of being extraordinarily special, such as receiving messages from God?
    4. Has he/she heard voices that command to behave in a directive fashion?

B.  Present mental illness (see above symptoms)

C.  Relationships with others
    1. Does he/she have a history of being a loner?
    2. Does he/she have any sustaining ties with other persons?
    3. Has he/she experienced the recent loss of an important relationship?
    4. Is he/she affiliated with militant political groups or "fringe" religious sects?

D.  Perceived grievance that has recently increased in significance.

E.  History of attempts to contact a protected person

F.  Current mental and physical capacity to develop a plan and act in a sustained, organized fashion to carry out that plan.

II.   Assessment of a Potential Assassin

If the above preliminary assessment suggests that a more formal assessment is in order, a variety of other factors should be considered.  Long-range prediction of what a particular individual will do may not be possible; it is possible, however, to anticipate short-range behavior in specific cases.  Rather than think about

95

dangerous people, we prefer to think about dangerous situations--situations involving a specific subject, a victim, and an act under specific circumstances. Therefore, our comprehensive evaluation attempts to ask questions about these factors; moreover, we have added items particular to identifying persons who might be dangerous to a president.

A. History and background of subject
   1. Family history
      a. Relationships with parents and siblings
      b. Relationship of parents to one another and to the family
      c. Family history of mental illness or violence
      d. History of subject's having been beaten or abused as a child
      e. History of subject's having had physical fights with parents
      f. Cultural background of subject and significance and importance of violence and/or assassination in that culture.
   2. Psychiatric history
      a. Attitude toward illness and helping agencies
      b. Wish to return to the hospital
   3. Present symptoms of mental illness
   4. History of suicide attempts
   5. Sexual history
   6. Criminal history

B. Action-producing conditions
   1. Episodes of excitement, accompanied by uncontrolled motor activity
   2. Delusions of having special powers or missions
   3. Voices commanding subject to behave in a particular fashion
   4. Delusions of transmitting and/or receiving devices having been implanted in one's brain
   5. Impulsivity
      a. History of accidents, automobile violations, bedwetting, fire setting
      b. History of antisocial behavior
   6. Substance abuse (alcohol, amphetamines, PCP [angel dust], barbiturates or "downers")
   7. Organic problems
      a. Temporal lobe epilepsy
   8. Episodes in which person feels separated from his/her actions ("It was like watching myself in a movie.")
   9. Existence of a delusional world inhabited by threatening persons

C. Interpersonal relationships
   1. History of only very few close friends, if any
   2. Inability to care for others
   3. Recent rejection by or loss of a loved one
   4. Perceived rejections and betrayals by persons
      in governmental organizations
   5. Difficulty at work with co-workers and/or superiors

D. Means
   1. Ability to travel to the protected person
   2. Ability to form and carry out a plan
   3. Easy access to a weapon

E. Setting
   1. Recent, well-publicized violent acts in the
      same geographic area as the protected person

F. Current life events
   1. Present stresses (social, economic,
      interpersonal, job-related)

G. Action
   1. Threatening letter(s) from subject to president
      or to Secret Service
   2. Visit from subject to White House or approach
      to president

An interview is the means by which clinicians and Secret Service agents obtain data about subjects; we have some specific recommendations about the setting, the interview itself, and the interview team.

## Setting

Agents who visit a subject at his/her place of residence will have an opportunity to see the living situation. Agents can sometimes make inferences about a subject's psychological state by seeing his/her personal environment. Such information can be quite valuable. However, we suggest that all interviews after the initial interview take place in the agents' offices. A setting more familiar to the agents, such as their offices, will allow them to be more comfortable and better able to elicit information from the subject. Whether the interview takes place at the subject's home or the agent's office, both agents and subjects should sit with equal access to doorways and exits. Agents should not sit between the subject and the exit, and should be careful to stay within the subject's view.

## Conducting the interview

The agents first should address the subject's interests and complaints. They will obtain more information if they agree with the subject's complaints and are appropriately sympathetic; however, they should avoid entering into the subject's psychosis or delusional system. They should follow the subject's verbal leads, listening but asking few questions. At the conclusion of the interview, direct questions about the subject's threats, intentions, plans, and means for carrying out the threats are important. Confronting and "stressing" the subject are generally unproductive; such techniques should be used only late in the interview and with the purpose of eliciting more information about the subject's thoughts and feelings about the protected person. The agents should be available to help the subject obtain assistance for his/her complaints, and may need to arrange for suitable psychiatric/psychological treatment. Following the interview, agents should record their impressions of the subject, paying particular attention to their own thoughts and feelings about the individual. These impressions are extremely important in drawing conclusions about that individual's potential dangerousness.

## Personnel

Male-female interview teams will provide substantially increased cooperation from the subject and will lead to richer data. We recommend that each subject, male or female, be interviewed by such a team. Consultation with mental health professionals can help these agents to develop the techniques of a team approach.

## III. Selection and Training of Agents

If we generalize from the agents we have met, we would conclude that the Secret Service chooses individuals who are likely to be effective in assessing subjects. In our view, an agent should be someone who is stable, relates well to others, has friends, possesses some self-knowledge, and is capable of tolerating and dealing with anxiety. He or she should be flexible in solving problems, curious about what makes people tick, and basically empathic. It is important that agents be people who can be appropriately suspicious and vigilant. The agent must be able to see his/her work as professional, having clear ideas about the job and keeping a sense of perspective. Moreover, agents should be able to think and respond quickly.

In our view, an agent should be somewhat compulsive, worrying about doing well enough, never too satisfied with yesterday's accomplishments.

Training for agents should include didactic education concerning mental illness. The content of training should include information about psychosis, affective disorders, character pathology, organic pathology, and drug and alcohol abuse. But no amount of didactic training can substitute for supervised, direct contact with mentally ill people.

Ways of training agents to assess mentally ill subjects include the following.

## Hospital-based training

Agents can participate in courses, interviews, and other clinical interventions to acquire basic diagnostic and interviewing skills.

## Training Academy-based instruction

Agents participate in time-limited workshops offered by mental health professionals. Workshops should be designed both for new and for more experienced agents.

### On-the-job training

Clinicians can join agents on occasional assignments and provide assistance, supervision, and consultation. The educational objectives of hospital-based training are to provide the agent with:

A. basic knowledge of different forms of psychopathology associated with unlawful behavior
B. basic knowledge and skills in clinical interviewing and intervention
C. understanding of the effects of mental illness on social and intellectual functioning
D. basic knowledge of factors causing impulse dyscontrol.

Agents should attend a seminar on mental health, mental illness, and dangerousness, observe clinical interviews, perform supervised clinical interviews, observe court-ordered evaluations of patients who have acted violently, and work on treatments units.

We suggest that hospital-based training occur in maximum security psychiatric facilities, which exist in most states, such as Bridgewater State Hospital in Massachusetts.

IV.   Composition of Agents Corps, Squads, and Interviewing Teams

The ethnic, racial, and gender composition of the agent corps should be a key issue for the Secret Service. Same-sex and same-race interviewers are likely to obtain different information (often more comprehensive and accurate) from subjects than are-opposite sex and other-race interviewers. Cross-racial and cross-sex squads and interviewing teams provide maximum flexibility with subjects, particularly with paranoid persons. Some women will talk more freely to a female agent; some women will talk more freely with a male agent. The same is true for male subjects. The Secret Service should consider how to recruit, select, train, and keep sufficient numbers of female, black, and Hispanic agents to meet the criteria above.

V.   Support of Agents

There is no question but that agents have exceedingly difficult and stressful jobs. As one agent explained to us, "If somebody calls the White House and threatens the president, we can get a call within minutes. We may have to go out immediately, interview the subject, talk with whatever family members we can find, and, within a matter of hours, report to Washington about whether the subject is dangerous to the president."

Agents provide peer group consultation and support for each other. Currently, there are too few opportunities for agents to consult with mental health professionals who are experienced at assessing and managing dangerous patients. If available, such consultation could:

A.   assist in quality control by adding a clinical voice
     to the decision-making process
B.   reduce some of the stress of the agent's job by
     decreasing the feeling (not necessarily valid) that
     one is making decisions outside one's training and
     expertise
C.   provide up-to-date knowledge for agents about local
     mental health resources
D.   build a network of mental health professionals who might
     hear of individuals who should come to the attention of the
     Secret Service

We propose that the Secret Service contract with outside agencies for mental health resource groups. Such groups could provide important consultation to the Secret Service in interviewing, diagnosing, assessing dangerousness, developing dispositional alternatives, training, and supervision. Members of a mental health

100

resource group would be available to agents on an as-needed basis. Need would be determined by the Secret Service, whose agents would initiate contact with the resource group.

Ten to twelve mental health resource groups would function as a national system.  Each would be based in a major population center and would work with the local Secret Service office.  Each group should be based in a mental health teaching institution.  Mental health and behavioral science professionals with experience with violent individuals would be available for around-the-clock consultation.  Resource groups should have adequate female and minority representation.  Groups should consist of sufficient numbers of persons to allow for reasonable sharing of responsibility, representation of race and sex, and speed of movement.  The broader the geographical area to be covered, the larger the group needs to be.  Resource group members should receive an initial orientation through the Secret Service and should meet together on an infrequent basis (perhaps no more than once a year) to discuss techniques, strategies, problems, new knowledge, and experiences.

VI.    A National Mental Health and Behavioral Science Advisory Group

In recent years the Secret Service has, by necessity, become a front-line mental health screening group.  Much of the work of agents involves interviewing, assessing, and attempting to find treatment for individuals who are mentally ill and who lack adequate treatment.  The current national policy of deinstitutionalization has placed many mentally ill individuals with histories of dangerous behavior into the community.  Many of these persons, in the past, would have been effectively contained in state-supported mental hospitals.  These patients often are difficult to treat.  They may be reluctant to accept needed medication.  Frequently they have neither treatment nor social supports.  Our experience suggests that this population will more and more frequently come to the attention of the Secret Service.  We think Massachusetts' experience can be generalized to the nation.

We propose, therefore, that the Secret Service appoint a national mental health and behavioral science advisory group.  This group should meet regularly with senior Secret Service staff to advise the Service on mental health issues and policies that affect its work, particularly policies concerning staff training and education.  It should keep the Service abreast of relevant recent research and should be a sounding board for the agency's internal research and assessment efforts. It would stand as a symbol of the Service's willingness to maintain contact with mental health and behavioral science professionals.  A national advisory group should consider recommendations for changes in national and state policies concerning individuals who are convicted of threatening Secret Service protectees.  It should advise the Service on how best to share information with state mental health officials about individuals who come to the Service's attention and should aid the Service in formulating policies on information-sharing.

VII.  Storage and Analysis of Data Relevant to the Service's Function

Although we are not intimately familiar with the Service's current method of organizing the information its agents collect, we have been told that there is need for change.  Agents report that several years ago, when the agent pool was much smaller, one knew most other agents and could gather and interpret information on a personal knowledge basis.  With the Service's dramatic growth in the past ten to fifteen years, such personalized data assessment is not possible.  Further, while the Service has thousands of files with information about subjects who have come to its attention, there has been no systematic effort to analyze these data in ways which might improve the Service's ability to find, assess, and manage such subjects.

We recommend that the Secret Service develop a standard investigation record and computer capability for making records accessible to agents.  We suggest that the Service ask its consultants to develop a research plan which would utilize both its internal data and data available from other sources.  The Service should have both internal research capability and the ability to contract for specific research.

We have outlined one model for a standardized investigation record and have included it in the Appendix.  This record would organize information directly related to the Service's goals of assessment and management.  The standardized investigation record should have the following elements:

A.  pre-coded format to allow efficient computer entry and analysis
B.  narrative entry spaces to permit concise verbal accounts necessary for reporting details, exceptions, qualifiers, and other important information not conducive to pre-coding
C.  ease of operation
D.  potential for periodic updating
E.  data source coding
F.  data verification coding.

Properly pre-coded, standard investigation record data could be entered on a computer within hours to days of collection, thereby quickly becoming available to Secret Service agents worldwide.  Such data can be gathered for each investigator to identify blind spots (such as missing data in the same categories too often) or bias (such as dispositions disproportionately correlated with one variable). These data, computer stored, could be a permanent and cumulative record of Secret Service investigations.

VIII. Memorandum on Potential Female Assassins

An interdisciplinary group of professionals met at McLean Hospital to discuss women as potential presidential assassins. Past efforts have focused on developing "psychological profiles" only of male assassins and threateners; our preliminary search of the literature has neither yielded such information about women nor references to the three women who have recently made attempts to kill a president. We know that the Secret Service must, by federal statute, investigate each threat upon the president and be concerned with identifying those persons and situations which are potentially dangerous. We believe, however, that a "psychological profile" of the potential female presidential assassin would not be useful; it would lead to overprediction, which is fruitless.

Also in our consideration is the fact that when women murder, they are more likely than men to kill their spouses. Almost half of their victims are spouses, and nearly all are family, friends, and acquaintances. Women kill people with whom they have a relationship. Although few women actually have a relationship with a president, he is not necessarily safe from attempts on his life by women. A woman may act in a dangerous fashion toward a president on behalf of a man with whom she has a relationship and/or on the basis of her fantasied or delusional relationship with the president.

When interviewing women suspects, Secret Service agents need to question these women about their relationships. They should focus on the woman's past and present family and love relationships and on her current living situation. Has she or a loved one recently experienced losses, rejections, financial or health problems for which she might hold a president responsible? The interviewers will also need to examine her real and/or unreal notions about her relationship with a president, and learn whether she links it to other important relationships from her past.

These interviews should be conducted in settings that are relatively free from tension or fear. A woman subject will generally be more comfortable, less guarded and suspicious, and more likely to disclose private thoughts and fantasies about men and about a president if she is interviewed by a woman agent; some women subjects, however, will respond more fully and frankly to a male interviewer. Because of this, each female subject should be interviewed by a man-woman team. These interview teams will provide substantially greater opportunities for an agent to use his/her particular skill, will elicit more productive data, and will greatly enhance the process of gathering clinical information for subsequent decision-making.

To implement these recommendations, the Secret Service will need to recruit sufficient numbers of female agents so that the teams can be developed. Frequent consultation and case review with a male-female mental health team will be helpful to the agents in maximizing the unique contribution of each agent while enabling them to work smoothly together.

Because women murder within the context of a situation and a relationship, the Secret Service should learn more about the target a woman selects. It is likely that some women may be dangerous not to presidents in general but to a president in particular. Since the actual numbers of women who have attempted to kill a president are so few, we suggest that the Secret Service examine attempts upon and threats toward other prominent public figures by women, followed by an investigation of threats toward and/or attempts upon the lives of congressmen, senators, and governors across the country. The investigation would involve interviewing women threateners and learning about their real and/or fantasied relationships with their targets, researching the behavior of the targets, and reviewing the characteristics of those prominent public figures who have never been threatened. A comprehensive investigation of women and their targets will yield important information for use by the Secret Service.


IX.   Recommendations

It is recommended that the Secret Service

1.  expand its training of agents with curricula to include hospital-based training in understanding mental illness and more knowledge of clinical interviewing

2.  develop teams of male and female interviewers for better understanding of women who threaten a protected person and for better understanding of male paranoid subjects

3.  increase the number of minority and female agents for purposes of expanding interview techniques and to communicate better with minority subjects who threaten a protected person

4.  develop mental health resource groups for consultation, disposition of threateners, training and supervision in the educational process of agents

5. develop a national mental health and behavioral science advisory group for study of mental health issues and policies to keep the Secret Service abreast of recent research data, and to recommend pertinent new research

6. develop a standard investigational record computer capability

7. improve research capability.


## APPENDIX

Standardized Investigation Record

A. Administrative (process) data, such as
   1. identifiers (name, social security number, identifying marks, aliases, date of birth)
   2. demographic data (age, race, sex, social class)
   3. address, phone numbers
   4. schools attended
   5. jobs held
   6. relatives' names and locations
   7. contacts' names and locations
   8. stage of investigation
   9. investigating agents
   10. dispositions
   11. initiation of report
   12. type of target of threats

B. Personal and family history data, such as
   1. exposure to violence in the home
   2. childhood behavioral patterns
   3. adolescent behavioral patterns
   4. personal psychiatric history
   5. personal medical history
   6. family stability data
   7. family medical history
   8. family psychiatric history
   9. family criminal history

C. Diagnostic category
   1. antisocial personality disorder
   2. schizoid personality disorder
   3. paranoid personality disorder
   4. narcissistic personality disorder

5. borderline personality disorder
6. sadism
7. pyromania
8. explosive disorder
9. obsessive-compulsive disorder
10. post-traumatic stress disorder
11. manic episode
12. major depressive episode
13. paranoid disorder
14. schizophrenia

D. Criminal history data including
   1. juvenile record
   2. school delinquency history
   3. military disciplinary history
   4. arrest histories (state, federal, Interpol)
   5. conviction history
   6. correctional history

E. Substance use and abuse history, including
   1. alcohol
   2. opiates
   3. stimulants
   4. sedative-hypnotics
   5. hallucinogens

F. Injustice history, including
   1. civil suit history
   2. complaining letter history
   3. complaining phone call history
   4. perceived injustice

G. Armament inventory, including
   1. knowledge of firearms and explosives
   2. books and manuals obtained from libraries
   3. magazines, books and manuals purchased
   4. subscriptions
   5. imagery of pictures owned and displayed
   6. weapons owned
   7. firearm registration and licensure
   8. access to explosives and munitions

H. Situational variables, including
   1. recent life stress
   2. recent substance use
   3. recent mood cycles
   4. geographic drifting or movement
   5. access to information on government leaders
   6. recent absenteeism from work
   7. current social network
   8. recent help-seeking behavior

# NOTES ON THE SECRET SERVICE AND THE PROTECTION OF THE PRESIDENT

Robert Michels, M.D.*
Barklie McKee Henry Professor of Psychiatry
Cornell University Medical College
Psychiatrist-in-Chief
The New York Hospital
New York, New York

## I.

The protection of the president, his family, and a number of other designated persons is a vital function of the Secret Service. The conceptualization of this task appears to have evolved since its initial formulation, starting with the immediate personal protection, or "bodyguard" function, and then expanding to include the response to threats and the screening and management of threatening persons. These latter activities now involve a considerable amount of Secret Service time and effort. However, before discussing this task and some possible approaches to improving its efficacy and efficiency, it might be interesting to speculate about the future possibilities in the evolution of the Service's mission. If the first phase was immediate protection and the second the screening and management of threats, a plausible third phase would be the identification of possible sources of danger and their evaluation. This would represent a continuation of the shift from a passive to a reactive and then to a proactive stance, with the task defined as maximizing the security of the person being protected rather than evaluating dangerous persons that come to the attention of the Service or thwarting actual attacks. Metaphorically, this would be analogous to a shift from first aid to the treatment of disease, and then to the public health concern with the cause and prevention of illness. It is possible that, as in the medical metaphor, the major threats to the president's security are not associated with those persons who come to the Service's attention, but rather with those who are not "referred" by the current network, and that an active program of identifying potential threats would be more productive than improved screening and evaluation of those threats that are now detected. We will return to this issue later.

## II.

Focusing for the moment on the current concept of the Service's mission, there are three functions that will be discussed: (1) the

---

*Commissioned paper

delineation of specific tasks and the formulation of job descriptions; (2) selection, retention, and promotion procedures for agents; and (3) training methods and curricula. The question of tasks and job descriptions arises because of the extremely varied and difficult tasks assigned to the Service. At various times agents must physically protect the president and others; interview and evaluate mentally ill individuals; maintain liaison with police, mental health institutions, the penal system, and others; and so forth. These tasks are sufficiently heterogeneous that the Service must decide whether its work will best be accomplished by "generalists" or "specialists," or, more likely, what should be the optimal ratio between the two. The answer to this question will, of course, change as the activities of the Service evolve, and care must be taken that the answer be responsive to the current definition of the Service's tasks, rather than reflecting an earlier, narrower concept or, conversely, anticipating future developments that have not yet occurred. The question can be illustrated by considering the advantages for the screening function of having agents with a wide variety of personal backgrounds and interests, and with extensive training in psychosocial and interpersonal skills, while the direct protective function would clearly lead to quite different priorities in selection. It is undoubtedly desirable to have a significant number of agents who combine the capacities necessary for both functions, but it might limit the excellence of the program if the roles were formulated in a totally "homogenized" way.

Shifting from job description to recruitment and selection, most of the experience of others in the selection and training of persons who are to interview, evaluate, or manage the mentally ill would suggest that recruitment and selection are at least as important as training. We are much more successful in identifying persons who have interpersonal sensitivity, empathy, or psychological mindedness than in training those who do not possess them. Put in other terms, training enhances these traits in those who already have them, but it has little impact on those who are initially low in them. Most persons who are experienced in teaching psychiatric interviewing place more faith in selecting the trainees than in constructing their curriculum. Psychologic and psychiatric interviews, group training exercises, assessment of psychosocial skills, and psychodiagnostic procedures should all be considered as selection tools. They would also provide the basis for an important future research project--the development of predictive criteria for identifying potential agents who will perform well or poorly at various tasks--and, therefore, for selecting future agents and assigning them to specific tasks. Indeed, if at present one agent were discovered to be particularly good or bad at screening potentially dangerous persons, it would be difficult to generalize this information usefully unless there were descriptive measures that would relate him to other agents in some consistent way. One might try to study what he did, rather than who he was, but the nature of the task is such that the study of "what" without "who" would be of limited value.

Training procedures will be discussed in three categories: education in psychologic and psychiatric knowledge; the development of skills in interviewing, assessment, and evaluation; and programs of continuing education. Although there is little certainty concerning what kind of knowledge would be most relevant, there would probably be reasonable consensus about where to start. Persons who will be evaluating the mentally disturbed should have some basic exposure to psychopathology, the major psychiatric syndromes, and simple principles of psychodynamics, with particular emphasis on factors related to impulsive or violent behavior--organic disturbances, sociopathy, manic, paranoid, and acute psychotic states, drug-related states, and so forth. They would also require knowledge concerning those conditions in which questions of impulsive behavior or violence might enter the differential diagnosis--obsessional or panic episodes, fugue states, and so forth. They would learn about suicide, homicide, violence, criminal behavior, and the group, social, and cultural aspects of such behavior. They would learn about the social networks in which persons with these problems exist--family and community, treatment institutions, penal institutions, and also about the various caretakers and professionals with whom they have contact. They would visit prisons and mental hospitals, and learn what they are like. They would learn about treatment programs, and the natural history of the major disorders, with particular emphasis on the persistence of paranoid fantasies in covert form. Finally, they would learn about the theoretical basis of interviewing--transference, defenses, projection, and so on.

Simultaneous with these educational experiences would be training exercises involving exposure to real subjects, similar to those who will later be evaluated, practice interviews, and so forth. It is essential that some of these exercises be conducted with real people, not actors simulating subjects or videotapes, although both of these may be useful adjuncts. The emotional stress of an interview on the interviewer cannot be replicated without involvement with real subjects. These interviewing experiences could take place in a variety of settings. One possibility would be a practicum, perhaps similar to the exposure of medical students on a psychiatry clerkship; another would be contact with selected patients, perhaps institutionalized, who are drawn from the population that will later be the focus of interest; a third would be accompanying experienced agents and participating in tandem with them as trainees. There would probably be an advantage to combining these, allowing the trainee a number of different views of the population under consideration.

An incidental problem is that of access to the subject populations necessary for training. I would see no ethical problem in providing this access. The difficulties that have been encountered might represent negative attitudes toward the Service among the various professions and disciplines who care for the subjects in institutional and other settings. If this is true, it probably has ramifications far beyond the question of training, which will be explored in more detail below. Some of the obstacles might be overcome by compensating volunteer subjects drawn from the population in question, a procedure that is consistent with ethical practice in the health professions.

Any comprehensive approach to training must include some type of continuing training, involving agents after they have completed their initial educational experiences. This could be in the form of periodic "brush-up" courses, ongoing clinical experiences while working in the field, visiting consultants, and so forth. There have been a sufficient number of new developments in our knowledge of psychopathology in the past decade to suggest that without such continuing input the effectiveness of agents in the field is likely to decay significantly over time.

## III.

A program of this scope and importance obviously requires ongoing development and evaluation. However, there are special difficulties here. One is attempting to prevent what is already a rare event, therefore, it is difficult to evaluate the effect of the prevention program. However, without some version of such an evaluation, there is no way to improve the program or to determine how many resources should be devoted to it. Therefore, an immediate problem concerns what types of partial evaluations or analog systems for evaluation can be developed.

The performance of individual agents can be evaluated by the use of standardized video interviews, direct observation in the field, or the use of actors unknown to the agent who simulate subjects in random field evaluations. These methods would determine whether agents are doing what they "should" be doing, probably to be defined as what experts and experienced agents think that they ought to be doing. It would not determine whether that consensus is valid, whether what they "should" be doing is in fact effective.

A second component that could be evaluated involves the selection and training procedures. The agents who emerge from given selection and training processes could be tested and compared with a control group selected by different criteria or trained by different methods. Systematic differences could then help in planning future selection criteria or curricula.

A third type of evaluation would involve the methods and criteria used in assessing subjects in the field. It should be relatively easy to establish reliability of various procedures, measure their redundancy, and so forth. Here again, the most difficult problem would be validity, and it is difficult to improve a process if one cannot determine how well it is working. However, it may still be possible to increase its efficiency, and probably to detect certain procedures that miss information that seems to have face validity. For example, if it were determined that challenging or confronting interviews with paranoid persons lead to an under-reporting of previous acts of violence, this would be of interest even if it were not possible to demonstrate that these persons are subsequently involved in additional violent acts.

Analog systems for testing procedures might be developed from the study of homicide, suicide, violent offenders, or terrorism. Each of these has problems, but each might provide an opportunity for studying various aspects of the prediction involved--impulse control, the specificity of targets, the time course of risk, psychosocial and stress "triggers," and so forth. For example, knowledge concerning what type of material in the mass media precipitated flurries of social violence might alert one to a subject who reported recent exposure to such material, while measures of impulse control that failed to predict when chronically depressed individuals made suicide attempts might be considered suspect in their ability to predict other types of violence.

IV.

Finally, I will return to my initial comments, the potential shift from responding to threats to identifying potential sources of danger. In doing so, I will present a relatively radical proposal, one that I myself respond to rather negatively, but one that seems sufficiently interesting to warrant discussion. At present, although most of the "referrals" to the Service who are eventually considered to be significant risks are persons who have or have had contact with the mental health system, there are few referrals from the mental health system itself. If this system knows, cares for, and follows the same persons who are seen and evaluated by the Service, it is interesting to consider why there is so little interaction between the two. It is, of course, possible that "referrals" from the mental health system would be of little value, but even this could not be established without study. It is also possible that such referrals would overrun the capacity of the Service. If such referrals were of little relevance, the easy solution would be to ignore them. However, if they were comparable to those now seen by the Service, but represented a significantly larger number of subjects, it would raise questions about the value of current procedures. It would be possible to establish answers to such questions by studying

111

relatively small communities and extrapolating to the rest of the country.

What factors deter the mental health system from making such "referrals"? One involves the ethical problems relating to confidentiality, though most mental health professionals believe that there is no major ethical dilemma if it is in the patient's interest to violate his confidentiality, and that it is generally in the patient's (as well as society's) interest to prevent a major crime of violence. While there may be no basic ethical issue here, there may be a problem of consciousness-raising, one that might be solved by statements from leading figures in the profession known to be interested in such issues. Secret Service policies that protect the confidentiality of information from informants, especially if it could be detrimental to the subject, might be helpful.

Related factors are the actual or perceived legal barriers to such "referrals." Professionals might fear that their patients will have legal claims against them if the patients' identities are disclosed to the Secret Service. The confidentiality and security of the Secret Service record system would be relevant here. In addition, legislation limiting such claims might be effective.

Probably the most important factor relates to prejudices and attitudes concerning the Secret Service. If the Service is seen as a police agency, it will be regarded with skepticism by mental health professionals; if it is viewed as concerned and competent in regard to the needs of those it evaluates, as well as those it protects--in effect as a kind of social service agency--the attitudes of mental health professionals might change. It is conceivable that the most critical information regarding potential danger to the president and related individuals is located in the mental health system, and that the most modifiable step in the protective process does not involve improving the selection and training of agents or the efficacy of screening procedures, but rather improving the referral system and the flow of information into the agency itself. A central issue might be the image of the agency, particularly with mental health professionals, and their willingness or even eagerness to cooperate with it. A modification at this step would have the effect of greatly increasing the scope of the agency's knowledge and extending its network of information, with the agency itself having a central monitoring function. There are clearly potential dangers to civil liberties in such a system, and it is probably the fear of such dangers that has prevented it from evolving. However, if these dangers are only potential and can be controlled, there are possibilities to be explored. Perhaps the most important thing that mental health consultants can do for the Secret Service is not to teach it how to train agents or evaluate and manage subjects, but rather to facilitate its becoming a specialized part of the mental health system, linked (with appropriate controls) to the rest of the system.

LEARNING FROM EXPERIENCE, THE SECRET SERVICE,
AND CONTROLLED EXPERIMENTATION

Lincoln E. Moses, Ph.D.
Professor, Department of Statistics
Stanford University
Stanford, California

1.    A True Fable

In the second half of 1980 a manager in a Washington
statistical agency noted that there was a small room, always filled
with four clerks using telephones.  Inquiry revealed that they were
telephoning recipients of questionnaires who were late in responding,
to remind them of their legal obligation to reply.  The clerks were
engaged in "follow-up of non-response."  The manager inquired, "Why
is this done?"  She was told, "To improve the response rate"--but no
facts existed about how well it worked.  So she (the manager)
required that half the names on the non-respondent list--chosen with
a table of random numbers--not be phoned at all that month.  Then the
timeliness of response in the two groups, called and uncalled, could
be compared and the benefits of phone follow-up weighed against the
costs.

The result was surprising.  Response was no better at all in
the group receiving telephone follow-up!  The four clerks were
assigned to more useful work.

This true story briefly illustrates the investigative and
convincing power of the experimental approach to resolving practical
questions.  The alternative, theoretical disputation over the merits
and demerits, can be endless; and when it does come to a conclusion
(right or wrong), it is likely to leave many unresolved doubts.  So
there is wisdom in asking about practical questions of importance,
"Is there some way to investigate this problem by a controlled
experiment?"

The answer necessarily is often, "No."  (The lung cancer and
smoking controversy would have been resolved much sooner if the
experimental approach could have been applied, but it could not.)

But the answer is sometimes, "Yes," and each such instance is
an opportunity that should be carefully explored.  Perhaps a direct,
convincing answer can be obtained to a nagging, unresolved doubt.

## 2. A Second Example and Some Discussion

The following idea was put to test in a celebrated experiment done in New York City in the 1960s. Idea: Arrested persons with community ties, such as jobs or homes in the locality, may safely be released before trial without posting bail.

All new arrest cases (excluding arrests for very severe crimes), over a period of many months, were interviewed before arraignment about their community ties (using a scoring system). Thousands of defendants were selected as "eligible," having high enough scores. The experimental staff then recommended, for pre-trial release without bail, a random half of those eligibles. The court accepted about 50 percent of these recommendations, and, in addition, released without bail about 16 percent of the eligibles in the random control half who had not been recommended. The results were that about seven-tenths of one percent of all the eligibles released without bail failed to show up in court. (Not everyone who does post bail appears in court.) This experiment showed so plainly the workability of the idea under test that it was directly applied routinely in New York City, and rapidly taken up in cities all over the country.

There was startling additional information turned up by the experiment. Among the eligibles, those chosen by lot to be recommended for pre-trial release without bail had a conviction rate of 40 percent, while those eligibles who were by lot not recommended had a 77 percent conviction rate! Further, of those who were convicted, 16 percent were sentenced to prison in the first group and 96 percent in the second! These unexpected results show a powerful handicap to arrestees who are not at liberty before the trial to arrange for their legal defense.

In both these experiments, the answers that emerged were convincing and had practical consequences. At base, both had the power to answer the question and to convince the skeptical, because their method was simultaneous comparison of two well-defined different procedures on cases of unquestioned comparability. When a difference occurs under these conditions, it is not easily explained away; it is likely to eventuate in action.

## 3. A More Detailed Look at the Method

A fuller analysis of the widely-used experimental approach reveals several essentials which deserve examining here. They can be listed and taken in turn.
   
A.  There must be two (or sometimes more) alternate ways of proceeding. In the first example, these were "phone" and "wait." In the second, they were "release without bond" and "detain if no bond is posted."

114

B.  The two procedures must be definitely described.
    Otherwise the results are hard to apply.  To define the
    procedures in terms of "the way Jones does it and the way
    Smith does it" won't do.  Even if Smith's results are
    clearly much better than Jones', we are left wondering how
    Smith does it, and how we shall adopt his method for wider
    use.

C.  The class of subjects to whom the treatments are
    applicable must be clearly defined.  This was particularly
    important in the bail bond experiment; persons arrested
    for very severe crimes were not eligible for possible
    release without bond.

D.  The relevant outcomes must be agreed upon in advance.
    These outcomes were the date of receipt of the
    questionnaire (in the first example) and appearing in
    court on the date set (in the second example).  The choice
    of a relevant outcome can sometimes be much more
    difficult.  In comparing training programs, shall we count
    test performance, job performance, job satisfaction, all
    three, or something else?

E.  Fair ways to measure outcomes must be specified in
    advance.  If the measurement involves judgment or any
    subjective assessment, it can be very important that the
    judge, or assessor, not know to which group a subject
    belongs.  (This is called "blind" assessment; it is not
    necessary with very objective measurements--such as scores
    in target practice, or results of laboratory tests.)

F.  The alternate procedures should be applied simultaneously.
    This simple precaution saves the investigation from being
    weakened by some unforeseeable change in a crucial
    condition part way through.  It assures that all kinds of
    things, associated with weather, work load, epidemics,
    hiring freezes, computer breakdowns, are automatically
    similar under the two conditions.  It may prevent
    endless dispute later because a host of possible
    explanatory differences are simply barred from entering
    the picture.  Both of the examples used simultaneous
    comparison.  If either of them had, instead, compared one
    period on one treatment to a later period on the other,
    there would be doubts.  In the bail bond experiment, many
    things could have changed over time--the kinds of cases,
    the personnel making the assessment of community ties,
    some of the judges.  Every such doubt would make the
    outcome less trustworthy, and less useful.

G.  A mechanically random choice should determine (separately
    for each subject) the choice of procedure applied.  This

115

is a key requirement. It best assures that the subjects will be comparable in the two treatment groups; it simply prevents conscious or unconscious bias from favoring one of the treatments. In the bail bond experiment, it was known that the arrestees recommended for release were no better (or worse) than those not recommended, because it was literally the luck of the draw that decided which particular eligible subjects received the recommendation. Randomization was also crucial to the telephoning example. Without that precaution, the supervisor of the clerks might have chosen for no-phone-call those respondents who usually had prompt responses, or those involving the largest telephone tolls, or the respondents which were smallest; in any of these cases, the outcome of the experiment would have been debated and the whole undertaking likely undermined by concerns about group non-comparability. These concerns were actually prevented from arising by the use of physical randomization.

4.    Possible Applications in the Secret Service

It is best to begin by recognizing that some kinds of questions, vexing to the Service, are not likely to be susceptible to resolution by experiment. "Who is dangerous?" "How does interaction with a fanatical group affect the probability of dangerous behavior?" Tractable questions, instead, may relate to those things the Service does and how it does them. The essence of the method is to try out two or more methods in a manner that allows firm conclusions to emerge. It is a way--a very good way--of learning from experience.

Some early steps (not necessarily in order):

A.    Choose a problem. Identify cases of existing intra-service diversity of practice on the same matter, and ask, "Why does this diversity occur?" Is it possible that some of these practices are definitely better than others? Since any well-run federal agency is likely to strive for uniformity of practice, ingenuity may be needed to find diversity. But there are ways to try:
(1) When a subject is transferred from one office to another, there is likely to be a change in the way that subject is handled. Are there patterns in such changes? Do they point to hypotheses worth examining?
(2) There may be certain decisions that explicitly call for the judgment of two or more agents. What are the operational controversies that are sometimes settled in this process? Do they raise any questions deserving systematic study for trustworthy answers?
(3) There may be very similar (but not identical) classes of situations in which different procedures are used. Two

116

or more such classes might be the subject of an experimental check-out of all the methods, used in combination with each of the closely-similar situations. Is there widespread internal dissatisfaction with any of the Services' present routines? Widely shared misgivings of a group of professionals, if objectively considered, may produce questions well worth experimental study. If work of some kinds is widely felt to be needlessly extensive, then it is likely to be widely ill-done. An experiment might settle the question of necessity and whether the result showed that an unpopular practice was, indeed, necessary or not. The answer, being definite, would be useful.

B. Identify measurable tokens of success or failure for outcomes. This step is best pursued in connection with the effort to explore a specific question. Still, some general observations may be possible. First, in attacking a problem experimentally, ask, "What outcomes do we hope will occur? What do we hope will not?" And "How can we track these outcomes?" Second, important outcomes may be of varied types, possibly ranging over such diverse matters as agent learning, quality of service from other law enforcement agencies, quality of contact with subjects, change in life style of subject, average time to complete an investigation, agent job satisfaction. Third, at points where reviews now occur (reviews of cases, of agents, of offices, of files) there may be opportunity to measure outcomes, and in terms already used by the Service.

C. Decide on fair outcome measures. Consider how to measure the outcomes in ways that cannot be distorted by opinions, beliefs, or wishes of participants. A frequently useful device is to have outcomes judged by qualified persons who do not know which experimental group any case is in (or, even better, do not know that there is an experiment going on).

D. Identify eligible subjects, cases, or opportunities. Specify the class of instances where either of the treatments under comparison may be legitimately applied in compliance with a random choice. Thoughts about this may lead to excluding in advance certain kinds of subjects (or cases, or agents) from the experiment.

E. Define the treatment precisely. Describe carefully the treatments to be compared. There can be allowance for flexibility, provided it is spelled out. For example, in medical experiments the dosage of a medication may be defined not as so many milligrams, but rather as the largest dose the patient can accept without nausea. Clear definitions of treatments can be challenging! A study about "the stress interview" isn't doable until that concept has been made more precise and also given a useful operational definition. Is the key feature the use of threat? Or refusing to be conciliatory when the subject voices distress? Eventually a characterization of two kinds of interviewing procedures may be achievable, where one clearly captures important components of the notion "stress interview" and the other lacks those, and where both types are definite enough to do or not do, unambiguously.

The foregoing list may seem formidable, and indeed the tasks there may demand much ingenuity and work. But the potential rewards are large. In the last 30 years, clinical medicine has made great strides, and it is fair to say that a large share of the success must be attributed to the widespread and persistent use of randomized, controlled clinical trials to securely establish good innovations and to drop poor ones. The complexities in medical applications are probably as great as those in the Secret Service setting. The Secret Service may do well to consider trying out the method.

5.    Some Strategic Suggestions

Start small and safe. Although an experimental study can be a simple matter (as with the telephone example), that is not likely. Murphy's Law will lurk. Hence the advice, take a "small" first problem, though a worthwhile one. If it has good prospects for success, so much the better, for that will facilitate attempting more controversial, more difficult, more important studies in later stages.

Even if a "small" problem is well chosen for its likelihood of success, and its realistic interest, that first attempt will be challenging enough! There are so many ways to go wrong: the treatment definitions can turn out to be fatally flawed, or some important outcome measure may only be obtainable in 70 percent of the cases, or the eligibility criteria for inclusion/exclusion in the experiment may overlook some numerous class of special cases. So method and discipline are essential throughout. But there is yet more challenge. It will be observed that the whole thing is easier to do if the treatments are not compared simultaneously, but in tandem. Yielding to this notion shoots the program in the head. Someone will notice that it is easier to use odd or even file numbers of new cases than to use random assignment. Yielding to this notion will probably allow someone somewhere to put new cases at choice into either treatment group, by jockeying the order of file number issuance.

Vigilance will be essential to prevent these and other modifications from ruining the first experiment. The point is that the essentials of the method are essential; there lies the challenge, to maintain those essentials.

There is so much potential value in the experimental mode of learning from experience that the Service may, after consideration, wish to ask interested members of staff, and some of its consultants, to propose one or more possible first studies. From among such proposals it would be very likely to see at least one attractive, initial study emerge.

# PROBLEMS IN ASSESSING AND MANAGING DANGEROUS BEHAVIOR: SOME COMMENTS AND REFLECTIONS

Saleem A. Shah, Ph.D.*
Chief, Center for Studies of Crime and Delinquency
National Institute of Mental Health
Rockville, Maryland

One purpose of the Institute of Medicine Workshop on Behavioral Research and the Secret Service is to help the Service augment its knowledge pertinent to its specific mission of protecting the safety of designated political figures and their families. To this end, it is necessary that the focus of attention not be limited solely to the prediction of dangerous behavior and the identification, assessment, surveillance, and management of potential assailants. We may have to direct our special attention and emphasis to potential assailants, but we should try initially to view the task in a broader perspective.

We are presumably in agreement that the behaviors of concern to this workshop are serious and potentially lethal attacks against the persons protected by the Service. What follows is a rough conceptual scheme that I would like to propose to the workshop participants as a framework for discussion.

The crucial behaviors of interest have three major elements, shown below, each of which is associated with key variables.

A. TARGETS (protected persons)
Characteristics
Availability
Vulnerability (e.g., risk-taking behaviors)
(Others)

B. ASSAILANTS (potential assassins and others)
Characteristics
Credibility and seriousness of threat posed
Presence and proximity
Lethal capability
(Others)

---

*I would like to acknowledge the helpful comments and suggestions of my colleagues Christopher Dunn, Thomas L. Lalley and Ecford S. Voit, Jr.

C.  SETTINGS, SITUATIONS, AND TEMPORAL FACTORS

Characteristics of settings and situations (e.g.,
the protected's usual place of work and residence,
temporary place of work and residence; in transit
situations, public and well publicized versus private
and unpublicized travel) and the risks associated
with each.

Temporary situations (e.g., political and other
crises during which risk potentials for some
governmental leaders may be appreciably increased).

Protectors (U.S. Secret Service and other protective
agencies, their key personnel, and their
capabilities) and the extent to which organizational
structure and operations of the agency facilitate
effective and efficient use of available resources;
availability of ongoing research and evaluation to
test the validity and effectiveness of assumptions
underlying various agency policies, procedures,
decision rules, training programs; factors that seem
to distinguish the "better" protective agents with
respect to specific roles, skills, and functions.

The following are some notions that follow from the above
conceptual scheme:

- Unless all three elements in the scheme (targets,
assailants, and settings/situations/temporal factors) come
together in space and time, there cannot be an
assassination attempt.  Moreover, even when all three
elements do come together, it is possible that the
presence and efforts of the protectors could help prevent
or thwart the attempt.  Therefore, appropriate control and
manipulation of any of the three elements in the scheme
could, in theory, serve to prevent an attack.

- Since there is no a priori reason for focusing attention
on any single element in the proposed conceptual scheme
(except for reasons of feasibility or practicality), all
three elements should be considered and kept in view in
any efforts to prevent an attack.

- If in particular circumstances one or another element and
its key variables is not amenable to needed manipulation
or control, then for purposes of preventing attack,
attention must necessarily focus on one or both of the
other elements and its key variables.  Targets and
assailants move about in space and time and must be

122

monitored and tracked. As for potential assailants, they must be identified beforehand.

● There are many technical, legal, constitutional, public policy and related constraints on the accurate identification and control of "suspected" potential assailants. The Service has (or should have) a considerable advantage over potential assailants in having both advance and highly accurate information about the location and movement of protected persons (at least in regard to events that are not publicized or part of public events such as inaugural parades and other public appearances of targets). Moreover, the Service can (or should) influence to some degree the nature and extent of advance publicity distributed about the movements of the protected, especially when unreasonably high risks are involved.

What follows are some further comments and elaborations on the elements of the above conceptual framework and a few of the key variables.

The workshop agenda indicates that the topics to be discussed focus primarily on factors associated with assailants. I have some serious reservations about the desirability and wisdom of this emphasis if the primary concern is to prevent assault on the protected. As the conceptual scheme makes evident, in order to prevent the criterion behaviors one must also remain very alert to the several other possible ways in which the Service's mission of protecting the safety of government leaders might be accomplished.

For example, I would argue that the characteristics (especially with respect to risk-taking behaviors) of the targets must also be considered when trying to assess the risks of assault.

A quick review of the few previous assassination attempts against presidents and presidential candidates, such as Robert Kennedy, makes it evident that these targets have almost never been attacked while in their regular or even temporary place of work or residence. Obviously, in such "regular" locations it is much easier to guard against assassination attempts. Similarly, in all the assassination attempts (with the single exception of the attempt on President Truman, when he was residing in Blair House), the targets were in some public setting. It would appear, therefore, that when the protected move around in public places they not only put themselves at considerably greater risk, but they may also be viewed by potential assassins as more vulnerable.

In light of the above observations, and considering the assessment of risk probabilities associated with the targets, especially when in public settings, one might wish to know: (a) Do the protected provide adequate information and notice to the Service about their various trips? (b) How much media and other advance publicity do the protected seem to desire in regard to trips that are associated with greater risk probabilities? (c) How willing are the protected to be guided by, or at least to seriously consider, the advice and suggestions of the Service with regard to reducing unreasonable risks associated with particular proposed activities?

Because our societal values pose various limitations in regard to controlling access to firearms and the kinds of surveillance measures that can be used, and because of the immense technical difficulties in making reliable and accurate predictions of events that have extremely low base rates, we should give much greater attention to the characteristics of the targets and to those situations in which assassination risks are greatly increased.

With regard to the foregoing, we might also distinguish between various types of constraints and limitations in terms of the available options for preventing or reducing risk probabilities of potentially lethal assaults on protected persons. For example, the constraints could be classified as technical (the state of predictive technology in regard to events that occur infrequently), legal and constitutional (such as prohibitions against "stop and frisk" searches, wiretaps, and the use of preventive detention of suspects), and political (the fact that elected government leaders would be reluctant to markedly reduce their exposure to the public).

The above classification makes it quite evident that there is not much that could be done about greatly improving predictive technology with respect to the accurate identification of potential assassins. There are also serious though not absolute limitations with respect to the legal and constitutional constraints. In theory, at least, assassination risks could be appreciably reduced by exerting greater control over the key variables under settings/situations/temporal factors, for example, by reducing and/or more closely controlling opportunities for assasination in public settings and situations.

Considering the tendency over recent years to increase the number of the protected, some attention should be given to identifying those who are of more critical "protective interest" and who are also at greater risk--at least judging from past data in this regard. For example, presidents appear, by far, to be at much greater risk while in office than after they leave office and as compared to vice presidents--whether during or following their terms in office. Such distinctions (which the Service probably already uses) are very essential in order that limited resources, personnel, and facilities be allocated in some relationship to degree of risk.

Along the same lines, it is unclear to me just how "major" presidential and vice presidential candidates are determined. Here, again, there are questions with respect to both national interest and risk probabilities. The more widely known candidates might be at greater risk of lethal attacks, while some other candidates might be more at risk for verbal abuse and beer cans.

There is yet another relevant issue of concern here. It is my impression that Congress has in recent years significantly increased the number of persons the Service has responsibility for protecting. Considerations other than perceived potential risk of dangerous assault seem to have motivated at least some of these enlargements. It would be worthwhile to consider whether the list of protected persons might properly be reduced--at least in reference to the responsibilities of the Service--in order that available resources be more carefully allocated for persons whose protection is much more a matter of national concern and who are also likely to be at greater risk. To the extent that sentiments of sympathy, concern, gratitude, and the like, appear to have motivated at least some of the additions by Congress to the list of protected persons, might not other and more appropriate expressions of such feelings be explored? For example, funds could be provided to designated persons in order that they might obtain desired or indicated private protective services; however, there would be no requirement that the funds so allocated could be used only for protective services.

Given the immense technical problems in trying to improve the predictive accuracy for events with extremely low base rates, Frank Zimring* has offered the excellent idea of considering "proxy validation" by the use of "plausible proxies." While this strikes me as a very good notion, the problem I have with the proxies presented is that their "plausibility" seems poor. Acts of interpersonal violence selected as proxies must have some functional equivalence, or at least close similarity, to the criterion behaviors of concern; otherwise, we would simply have exchanged one serious problem (very low base rates, or low frequency events) for another one (inability to extrapolate findings to the criterion behaviors of prime concern). Violent crimes in general, child abuse, spouse abuse, and suicide attempts strike me as being rather different and distinct from violence that is directed at national political leaders.

There are several other approaches that might be considered for dealing with the base rate problem and the difficulties in trying to analyze and make more sense of the very few cases available.

---

*Professor of Law, University of Chicago, in a memorandum to conference participants, included in this summary, page 187. A member of the planning committee, Mr. Zimring was unable to attend the conference.

First, assuming that violence directed at political leaders is in some ways rather distinct (i.e., assassination attempts), why not increase the rate by including serious assaults directed at state and perhaps even local political leaders? Of course, even though the targets would remain in the same descriptive category (political leaders), it is quite possible that only some of the attacks against state level politicians, and even fewer against local politicians, would be sufficiently similar to those against national political leaders.

Second, because protecting national political leaders is a concern that most assuredly is widely shared with most (if not all) other countries, one could undertake some cross-national studies and pool relevant data from several other countries, preferably from the Western democracies with socio-political characteristics similar to those in the United States. Moreover, once assassination attempts are classified into specific categories, such as mentally disordered assassins and politically-motivated assassins, it is possible that an even wider range of functionally equivalent incidents and cases could be pooled for study and analysis.

Third, might not the New York City Police Department have some relevant data in regard to their protective responsibilities for members of the various United Nations delegations and also with respect to foreign officials at the various consulates?

Fourth, it would appear that various other national leaders (non-politicians) may well have some of the same stimulus qualities as political leaders in attracting certain types of assassins (e.g., Martin Luther King, Vernon Jordan). Similarly, might attacks against some other public figures, such as John Lennon, also have some relevance?

There is one other conceptual approach that occurs to me in regard to efforts to deal with the base rate problem. We could try to consider the criterion behavior along a spectrum, where the "core" or prime behavior is first defined and identified, as in a well-planned and potentially lethal attack on a political leader. Then one could move out to less lethal attacks and attempts directed at the same general target group. For example, various types of attacks could be scaled and rated along some dimensions relevant to the critical behaviors. The seriousness or lethality of the attack might be one such dimension; being within good shooting range of the target with a loaded firearm would receive a very high rating, as would being within throwing range with a live grenade or some other explosive. An assault with a rock or other heavy object would have a lower rating, depending upon the pitching arm strength and range of the attacker, and so forth. Attacks with fists, sticks, or empty beer cans would be too far removed from the prime criterion behaviors and might either receive a very low rating or be excluded.

126

Finally, some brief comments about the protective and related capabilities of the U. S. Secret Service. It will have been noted that this appears as one large sub-category of variables under settings/situations/temporal factors in the conceptual scheme. As I had occasion to indicate in my first meeting with Mr. Robert Kyanko of the Secret Service, the agency simply must significantly increase and improve its capability for undertaking a range of in-house research efforts. There must certainly be a wealth of information that has been accumulated over the years with respect to threats, attempts, attacks, and so forth, against various persons protected by the Service. To what extent has such data systematically been analyzed and studied? To what extent have the operating procedures, various decision rules, intuitive judgments, training procedures for agents, and so on, been subjected to careful empirical assessment?

For example, a comparison of threats, attempts and completed assault in reference to a host of operational, situational, and other dependent variables might help provide some better and clearer idea of the risk probabilities associated with certain types of serious attempts and potentially lethal attacks. It might also be possible to try to pinpoint certain factors, such as lack of prior information, ineffective response by various protectors, or risk elements that have been overlooked, that seem to contribute to less successful protective efforts.

The Service also should have funds to support a variety of extramural research efforts that are directly relevant to its mission. As far as more basic studies are concerned on predictive technology more generally and related topics of broader concern, the Service might well wish to consider cooperative or joint efforts with other federal research support agencies.

In order to markedly strengthen its internal research capabilities in the behavioral and social science areas, and also to give this function much greater priority and emphasis than appears to have been the case in the past, there might be established a research advisory committee to assist the agency in developing, further improving, and maintaining at a high level its internal research capabilities. Members of such an advisory committee would be separate from the regular and direct research consultants that have been used from time to time and who should continue to be used as needed by the Service.

Finally, I would like to note that, in order that the available resources and capabilities of the protective branches of the U. S. Secret Service be used in the most effective and efficient fashion, it might be necessary to consider whether the organizational structure of the agency actually facilitates efficient functioning in regard to the key mission of concern. The analogy that comes to mind is that the potential horsepower of an automobile engine may not matter very much if, in actuality, the power is not efficiently getting to where--as the saying goes--"the rubber meets the road."

# PREDICTING VIOLENT BEHAVIOR: A REVIEW AND CRITIQUE OF CLINICAL PREDICTION STUDIES

John Monahan, Ph.D.
Professor of Law and Professor of Psychology
University of Virginia Law School
Charlottesville, Virginia

In looking at the state of the art in the area of predicting violent behavior, I will briefly review the clinical prediction studies. To my knowledge, there are only six studies which test the validity of predictions made by mental health professionals (clinicians) in the area of violent behavior. Five of them are reviewed in the monograph that has been distributed to all of you* (and are summarized on page 48), and one has been published since the monograph went to press.**

The level of accuracy in the predictions found in the existing studies ranges from 14 to 41 percent, with many different factors affecting the specific figure, most notably the base rate for the violent behavior in the population being studied.

The study that reported the highest percentage of "true positives" (41 percent) also had the highest percentage of "false negatives" (31 percent). ("True positives" are persons predicted to be violent who did, in fact, subsequently engage in the violent behavior. "False negatives" are persons predicted to be safe who turned out to be violent.) So there was a 10 percent differential in favor of the individuals predicted to be violent.

A fair summary statement of the existing literature on the prediction of violent behavior would be that mental health professionals are accurate at best in one out of three predictions of violent behavior that they make. Many reasons can be offered for this figure, perhaps the one most often cited being the low base rate problem—the fact that in many cases the violent behavior of interest

---

*J. Monahan, The Clinical Prediction of Violent Behavior, U.S. Department of Health and Human Services, National Institute of Mental Health (DHHS Publication No. [ADM] 81-921), 1981.

**E. S. Rofman, C. Askinazi, and E. Fant, "The Prediction of Dangerous Behavior in Emergency Civil Commitment," American Journal of Psychiatry 137 (September 1980): 1061-1064.

occurs so infrequently in the population under study that the error rate will of necessity be high. There are also many psychological factors that have been mentioned as accounting for the preponderance of "false positive" predictions generally (that is, predicting that an individual will engage in a behavior, when in fact he does not engage in it--in this case, a type of violent behavior), most important among them that the "costs" of the two types of mistakes--false positives and false negatives--are drastically different for the people doing the predicting. The costs of false negatives are generally much higher.

There are several observations that have to be made regarding the existing body of literature on prediction of violent behavior. One is that all the studies, with the exception of the one that was just recently published, involve long-term predictions. The persons predicted to be violent had all been in institutions for at least several months, and in some cases many, many years--15 years on the average in one study. They were followed up in the community for between three and five years. So these are not studies of violence that is about to take place imminently. They are studies of persons who have generally been off the streets for a long time--predictions about how they will behave when they are back on the streets for a long time.

Second, all the persons predicted to be violent in these studies were diagnosed as mentally ill. To what extent these findings can be generalized to people not diagnosed as mentally ill is not known. Third, all the persons predicted to be violent in these studies had a history of violent behavior in their background--often an extensive history of violent behavior--which meant that the base rates for violent behavior among this population were already higher than expected in the population at large. To what extent one would get predictive accuracy rates approaching one out of three in populations that did not have such a high base rate for violent behavior is unknown.

The existing research can be criticized on many grounds. The principal, and I think most serious, criticism is that the criterion that is used--arrest for violent crime, civil commitment for dangerous behavior, or, in some cases, an aggressive act noted on a hospital record--may in fact underestimate the actual occurrence of violent behavior. Thus, violent behavior may be occurring; it simply has not been found. So the question is, How many of the false positives are really true positives in disguise? This is a question that could be debated at length. My conclusion is that the existing research provides reasonable estimates of the accuracy of clinical predictions of violent behavior. It is likely, I think, that much of the unreported or unsolved violence is actually committed by those people who are arrested or civilly committed for other violent acts.

Thus it is not so much that the false positives are really true positives in disguise, but rather that the true positives are actually truer than we might imagine. Not only might they have done what they have been accused of doing or what they admit to doing, but much other violence as well.

In the monograph that Saleem Shah of NIMH commissioned me to write, I tried to systematize the clinical prediction process by providing a list of questions that clinicians might ask themselves in terms of how to structure an examination to determine the violence-potential of an individual. I would simply emphasize one point here: an examination of what situations or contacts appear to have elicited violent behavior in the past for any person and how likely is it that he or she will confront the same kinds of contacts and situations in the future might, indeed, be a very important factor to analyze in assessing that person's potential for violent behavior in the future. While mental illness in general, for example, does not, from the research, appear to be significantly related to violent behavior, in any given person case, a certain form of mental illness may be part of a pattern that sets the stage for violent ways of coping with life stress. In another individual, the presence of mental illness might be part of a pattern that leads the person not to be violent. I think, then, that the question is not so much whether various factors in general are related to violent behavior; but, rather, whether in specific cases, patterns can be found where a situation that the person is in tends to elicit violent ways of coping with the stress presented by that situation.

In my opinion, it is important for Secret Service agents to be aware of the literature on the clinical prediction of violent behavior. There may be clues in that literature relevant to the assessment of violence against protected persons. Certainly the methodological issues are similar--concerning true and false positives and base rates, for example--but, as I mentioned in my memorandum distributed to you, the predictors of political violence--of violence against protected persons--may not be at all synonymous with the predictors of street violence, and it has been street violence that has been studied in the literature: murder, rape, robbery, aggravated assault. I am really struck by the fact that some factors that seem to be strongly implicated in street violence seem not at all to be implicated in political violence. Race is the most obvious example. Every account of street violence heavily implicates race as a factor predisposing toward violent crime; yet, I do not know of any black presidential assassins, for example. Race seems either not to be involved in political violence, or to be involved in a manner opposite to the way it is involved in street violence.

Perhaps what is really called for with regard to Secret Service assessment procedures is two assessments. Stage one assessment might be an evaluation of violence potential, without regard for the identification of the possible victim. For this assessment, the existing prediction research is relevant. Stage two assessment might be called victim assessment, in which the "direction of interest" of the individual being assessed receives special attention. Perhaps it is at this second stage, where things like political ideology, membership in groups wishing to overthrow the government, and attribution of the sources of the stress in one's life to political figures are most relevant, rather than in the first stage of assessment for violence potential.

# ON INTERVIEWING POTENTIALLY DANGEROUS PERSONS

Shervert H. Frazier, M.D.
Psychiatrist-in-Chief
McLean Hospital
Belmont, Massachusetts

I, too, have thought about the various questions that have been raised here because most of our experience is based on assessing individuals who have crossed the personal assault line--who have killed someone, who have demonstrated dangerous behavior, and who are also mentally ill and in institutions for the mentally ill.

We could start out by noting that the Secret Service has various types of persons to protect, and not just the president who is now in office. In fact, most of the agency and staff energy are devoted to protecting a large number of other persons. The list of protected individuals has been expanded gradually over the years, so that what may be appropriate for use in examining or assessing and interviewing a subject about a president now in office may be different from what is appropriate for a protected person who is out of office, or one about to lose his or her protected status.

There are, also, some conflicts from my point of view about what the Secret Service agents have to accomplish. They have to obtain a lot of demographic data in the initial interview-- citizenship status, residence, changes of residence, employment, military service, aliases, and so forth--which they have to report back and which they must keep updated. Obviously they also need to find out about any mental or criminal history, education, training, skills, weapons knowledge, addictions, sexual-affectional preferences, family history and, more importantly, the specific ideation the individual has about the protected person.

Obviously there are volumes and volumes about interviewing techniques, interviewing skills, and interviewing methodologies, written for general interviewing, psychiatric interviewing, and so forth. Probably the most pertinent here is Merton's work on focused interviewing.[1] Although the book is old, some parts are relevant to Secret Service assessments of potentially dangerous subjects, as the subjective experience of a particular person in a given situation is discussed. Merton also discusses the dyadic and triadic interview situation, and the fact that the number of persons present during the interview is an important factor. The book is thus relevant to Secret Service considerations as to whether interviewing should be

done one-on-one or by pairs of agents with a subject.  Then, of
course, the subsequent writing of Kahn and Cannell[2] at Michigan
describe the communication process--the individuals receiving the
messages--and the problems involved in these communications, and the
various judgments which go into that dyadic or triadic situation.
There is also the MacKinnon and Michels book on the psychiatric
interview,[3] which essentially takes each particular diagnostic
category and describes the psychopathology and then proceeds to show
how to open the interview, how to manage it, what to expect, and what
kinds of questions to ask in an enlightened fashion, so that the
greatest amount of information is elicited in the shortest period of
time.

When it comes to what I do when I sit down with someone who is
said to be dangerous--said to have a threat in mind--I want to know
what is on the person's mind.  I work in a male hospital for the
criminally insane, but which is staffed with a large number of women
who are very important to the process of determining what actions and
interactions take place.  We always have a woman in the room during
the interview; she may be a nurse, a social worker, a psychologist,
or a psychiatrist.  I start out by trying to settle the person down
and inform him of the who, why, where, and what is going on.  This
has to do with being appropriately direct and at the same time not at
all misleading the patient.

When we communicate with Secret Service people, we note they
are very direct about what they are doing, and that is important.  I
don't know how they came by it, but intuitively they have learned to
keep aloof in interview situations--not to be buddy-buddy and not to
get too close to the very disturbed, the very paranoid person.  I
think this is an essential part of that kind of process.  They
certainly have been doing a good job with the mentally ill, at least;
and sometimes I think the question of feeling inadequate about what
one does is probably related to the factors which I will talk about
in a little while.

I always state the obvious:  what I am doing there and what I
expect to find.  I assume, also, that there are no secrets.  That is
the position I put myself in so that I can try to find out any
information and be open to ask any question that I think is
necessary.  I am also wary of prejudgments--fixed ideas on my part of
what this client is up to or what I think is in the offing for him.
This helps avoid stereotypes about what one anticipates from the
person one is interviewing.  I believe this is very important.

I don't always assume that a subject's interest in a protected
person (the president, for instance) is menacing.  The interest may
simply reflect the individual's need at a specific time.  Sometimes
the nature of that interest can best be extracted by eliciting the
strengths of that person in a very straightforward way. That is, not

everyone who is concerned about the president or the president's wife (as in the case described last night) has sinister intent. A good many people are concerned about them and have very long and detailed fantasies about them as authority figures, as individuals who represent persons out of their past, and I think that is an important part of what does happen.

The role of the Secret Service agent who is doing the interview may be quite different from the role of the physician who does an interview. In my view, the identity or role assumed by the agent is important. Do you, a Secret Service representative, think you are part of the criminal justice system, or do you think you are part of the mental health system when you are asking questions of persons? I know that you, also, encourage and participate in long-term care of persons who have made threats. The question is, What is your role identity in this? It is pretty important to get that straight so that you know which system you represent. One can use dignity and respect in either role, but certainly a police or criminal justice role and a mental health role are different. It is a special task which you have, to be sure. Since your statistics show that the majority of the persons you see are mentally ill, you are obviously into the business of evaluating the mentally ill and taking care of them or recommending some kind of care.

It is important in any interview situation that the interviewer pay attention to the following questions: Am I tuned in or am I being misled or getting confused? Is the situation not clear? The response to each is a visceral reaction and also a mental reaction to what is going on. That kind of awareness is essential to being tuned in and recognizing all the time that one must not enter into a persons's delusions or unrealistic expectations. It is also essential to be pragmatic, to keep one's mind on what is real.

Individuals being interviewed utilize symbolic references, symbolic ideas. They distort ideas. They avoid some things. They block in certain instances. And they often have a private logic. All of these things require careful determination.

I like to elaborate on the thinking processes of the person being interviewed. I like to know how concrete he is in his ideas. The degree of concreteness has something to do with the ability to carry out such ideas. I do this by putting a temporal frame around an event when a person is suspicious about something and I ask him, "Where were you when you first had that thought?" That essentially helps him come back to a place in space and he can begin to concretize. Then I do what is called a "micro interview," going into minute details to obtain a sample of an idea that was conceived and elaborated on during a given period of time. This leads to the very often unwitting demonstration of feelings about the situation being discussed. It also helps to build the data base on which to make a judgment.

I am interested, also, in persons with memory defects about these particular events because that, also, brings in the whole question of drugs and alcohol and amnesia and other kinds of repression which go on in a number of persons, especially paranoid individuals.

I do not push early in the interview for data when the person cannot deliver the data. I reserve that for later or for a subsequent interview.

I know that sometimes the Secret Service agent must be concerned with the time element. This may be the only opportunity to meet that particular person.

I have watched a number of people interview, and those who pace themselves to be insistent and persistent with the interviewee are able to induce stress without relying on an overt stress type of interview. I am aware that there are gradations of stress in any dyadic or triadic situation. The introduction of a self-recognized persistence which leads to a certain amount of stress has something to do with the kinds of data which come forth.

I also confront the person's dangerousness. When someone is dangerous I think it is often wise to let him know that we consider him dangerous, why he is dangerous, .that we have concerns about him, and that we want to stay in touch with him. This has to do with correcting reality. For very many people this approach rearranges their perception of what is going on and their impact upon other persons. I have found this tactic useful.

Obviously, when there are other psychological barriers, such as language or race barriers in the interview, there is no question that specialized interviewers from the particular language or racial/ethnic group are essential. This also applies to female clients, and the need for female interviewers, as we have outlined in our paper.

Knowledge of the psychopathology of various kinds of persons is helpful in pinpointing what to track down and what their specific defects are. For instance, if you are looking at schizophrenic persons, you question whether they have problems of personal identity, problems of dependency, problems with assertiveness or aggression or a struggle for power and control, and other defects usually present in this disorder. This helps in determining the kinds of questions that are important to ask.

The persistence of ideational patterns and the distortions of perception of the here and now are important in identifying the difficulty. I also note the recurrence of fixed delusional patterns in assessing behavior. We recently found at Bridgewater an extremely high number of persons who, in manic states, have the potential of being very dangerous. We also assess suicidal risk, because in the last analysis the suicide-homocide axis is very often intertwined.

I would like to caution Secret Service agents about investing too much expertise on the part of professionals. I think that very often you resort to physicians and psychologists and mental health workers in a hospital setting and are relieved that you have the assailant under wraps. I want you to know that your relief is false--that you probably know more about dangerous people than those mental health professionals in that particular situation.

## Notes

1. R. K. Merton, M. Fiske, and P. L. Kendall, The Focused Interview (Glencoe, Ill.: Free Press, 1956).

2. R. L. Kahn and C. F. Cannell, The Dynamics of Interviewing (New York: Wiley, 1957).

3. R. A. MacKinnon and R. Michels, The Psychiatric Interview in Clinical Practice (Philadelphia: Saunders, 1971).

# PROBLEMS AND METHODS IN PREDICTING PAROLE BEHAVIOR: UTILITY OF PREDICTION INSTRUMENTS

Don M. Gottfredson, Ph.D.
Dean, School of Criminal Justice
Rutgers University
Newark, New Jersey

John Monahan already mentioned that problems and methods of prediction in areas such as parole are no different generally from problems of prediction in other areas.

There is a long line of studies in the prediction of parole behavior, going back at least 50 years. Quite a lot has been learned in those studies. I shall mention about 10 or 12 things that may have some relevance to the concerns we are discussing. I assure you that there is good evidence for some of what I will have to say, but there is quite a bit of opinion mixed in, too. (I am not going to have time to tell you which is which!)

Some fairly stable predictors of parole behavior have been identified. These include such variables as the type of offense of conviction, age, indices of prior criminality or conviction, and drug abuse. These tend to be found repeatedly in many studies and to be fairly stable over time. At the same time, items of data that we might think would be useful in prediction turn out not to be. That is, there is simply a great deal of information on offender attributes that is not predictive.

It has been found that valid parole prediction devices can be developed. It has also been found that quite a lot of modesty in describing the degree of validity that we are talking about is in order. Also, despite our knowledge of how to devise predictive instruments (that is, statistical prediction devices), corrections agencies, probation departments, and similar agencies often fail to use widely accepted procedures in constructing them. Fundamental errors of method are made repeatedly, concerning such issues as representative sampling or the need to test validity in new samples before application or operational use of the instrument.

In the area of parole behavior, the evidence about clinical versus statistical prediction is much the same as in other fields. There has not been a lot of study in this particular area, but generally the statistical methods have fared better when pitted against clinical predictions.

One thing that has been learned more recently, from much debate and discussion about particular statistical methods for combining information into some kind of instrument, is that the more sophisticated statistical methods (and even more appropriate statistical methods with respect to the statistical theory involved) do not seem to work any better than much simpler methods.

It should be mentioned that the statistical literature on parole shows little or no ability to predict person offenses as distinct from property offenses. Although something is known about transitions from one offense to another when there is recidivistic behavior, one cannot predict the nature of the next offense very well from the prior offense.

It can be claimed that there are three areas of demonstrable utility for predictive instruments of the sort mentioned above. I will mention them in what I think are the rank order of confidence that I would have in the appropriateness and utility of their use. It might be a different order than you would suspect. The main utility, I think, for instruments of this sort is as a research tool in program evaluation studies in which there is a lack of appropriate experimental controls, such as randomization. Prediction methods provide some ability to correct for demonstrable bias at the start of the comparison. This may make possible a useful quasi-experimental design; and that is, in my opinion, the best use of this kind of instrument. A second use of this kind of instrument is in program planning. A third would be for placement decisions in cases where this kind of instrument is believed useful.

One of the things that has been learned from this line of investigation is that there is a need--if there is to be a serious attempt to investigate the potential usefulness of such a tool--for a research capability within the organization of the agency that will use it. There are a variety of reasons for this. One relates to the quality of the data that will be available. It is necessary to monitor the reliability of the data items. Another concerns the need to assess validity repeatedly, to see whether the empirically demonstrated relationships remain constant with the passage of time and with social change. Thus, the agency must have an ongoing, continuous evaluation program or function.

Finally, as discussed in John Monahan's monograph, it might be in order to move away from comparing the usefulness of clinical versus statistical prediction to examining the utility of statistical prediction via clinical prediction.

Based on this literature I would say that the most relevant issues to discuss in this conference are strategies for dealing with the base rate problem, the need for systematic data collection for this kind of research effort, and the idea that the development and continuing program should be located within the agency.

## Bibliography

1. Gottfredson, D. M. Assessment and Prediction Methods in Crime and Delinquency. Appendix K to the Task Force Report: Juvenile Delinquency and Youth Crime of the President's Commission on Law Enforcement and Administration of Justice, 1967.

2. Gottfredson, S. D., and Gottfredson, D. M. " Screening for Risk, A Comparison of Methods." Criminal Justice and Behavior 7 (1980): 315-330.

# SUICIDE AND SUICIDE PREVENTION RESEARCH

James H. Billings, Ph.D., M.P.H.
Director, Institute of Epidemiology and
Behavioral Medicine
San Francisco, California

Research problems presented by the low base rate for assassination have been raised several times in our discussion thus far. Some of the issues in suicide and suicide research provide interesting and informative parallels which may be relevant here. For example, suicidologists have been involved in attempting to identify the suicidal patient who ultimately kills himself or herself since Durkheim's Le suicide established a beginning for systematic investigation of suicidal behavior in 1897.

The suicide death rate in the general population is approximately 10 per 100,000, or .0001 percent. The rate of suicide among the highest risk group, previous suicide attemptors, is roughly 1,000 per 100,000 per year, or one percent. While one percent is a more researchable base rate figure, the reality continues to be that there are 99 chances out of 100 of being wrong in attempting to predict who will suicide even among the highest risk population. Prediction of suicide continues to be a complicated and controversial issue.

There are also similarities between suicidal patients and those exhibiting "dangerous behavior" in terms of management issues. What does one do legally, ethically, and therapeutically once the high risk person has been identified?

One of the most creative approaches to the prediction and management problems raised by the suicidal patient is exhibited by a study conducted in San Francisco by Dr. Jerome A. Motto.* This prospective study (1968-1974) followed 3,006 high-risk patients who were hospitalized at nine psychiatric inpatient facilities in San Francisco for a depressive disorder, suicidal ideation, or a suicide attempt. Each patient was evaluated by research associates, and 175 variables were coded on a research protocol for each case. All patients were followed up to five years after discharge to determine suicide or non-suicide status.

---

*J. A. Motto, "The Psychopathology of Suicide: A Clinical Model Approach," American Journal of Psychiatry 136 (April 1979): 516-20.

There were basically two purposes in conducting this study. One was to generate statistical models whereby it would be possible, with greater sensitivity, to identify the persons among the high risk group who were most likely to kill themselves. Second, the study was developed to test a suicide prevention technique designed for those patients who had declined to participate in mental health treatment following discharge. The findings of this study provide some encouraging perspectives on the problem at hand.

Dr. Motto has been able to generate two relatively successful predictive models, and others are in the process of being created. The ultimate value of this approach can emerge only through repeated prospective application.

This experimental suicide prevention program involved unobtrusive, non-demanding contact maintained with a random sample of the patients who had refused treatment after discharge. It consisted of a telephone call or letter which communicated an interest in how they were doing and expressed the hope that things were going well. The contact was maintained at regularly scheduled intervals for five years following discharge. It is my impression that there is a statistically significant difference between the contact and no-contact groups in terms of suicidal outcome.

The study described above suggests that there may be therapeutic value in using contact maintenance procedures for persons identified as "dangerous" by the Secret Service. That is, there is likely to be significant preventive value in providing the "dangerous person" with consistent and basically non-threatening contact with an organization, even the Secret Service.

# ASSESSING THE CREDIBILITY OF NUCLEAR THREAT MESSAGES

Brian M. Jenkins
Director, Security and Subnational Conflict Program
Rand Corporation
Santa Monica, California

One of several research projects on terrorism that we at Rand have been involved in over the years deals with assessing the credibility of nuclear threat messages. During the past 10 years in the United States there have been more than 50 communications--most of them written, a couple of them verbal--involving nuclear threats against American cities and including some sort of demand or message.

The problem in reacting to these messages is that the two traditional modes of assessing them are declining in utility. One was to dismiss them because we had confidence in the integrity of our safeguard system for nuclear materials. If no one can get the nuclear material, no one can make a nuclear device. However, there is an increasing amount of material in that system that is unaccounted for. More important, there are more and more nations which have their own nuclear programs. So there is a lot of nuclear material out in the world that is beyond the control of our inventory system, and therefore that method of dismissing a threat is less reliable. The second criterion of assessing such messages had to do with the technical quality of any diagrams, jargon, descriptions of devices included with the nuclear threat. As I am sure you have all seen in the newspapers, it has become fashionable for college students to design atomic bombs instead of writing term papers. Given public discussion of nuclear matters, those things which were once closely guarded secrets are now available to a much larger population; and we see more sophisticated messages which use nuclear terms correctly.

Therefore, it was considered necessary to develop a systematic capability for assessing the credibility of those messages. What is important here--and I think interesting about our study in the context of this conference--is that we are talking about assessing the dangerousness of an individual. We are talking about the credibility of a threat made by an individual to carry out a very specific act. That takes into account a broad range of facts and attributes about that person--not just his mind set, but also evidence of certain capabilities, and so on.

We were asked at Rand to develop the behavioral component of this threat assessment capability. (Others handle the technical and operational aspects.) We look at the message and try to provide information about the individual himself, about his mind set. We try to address the issue of credibility. I should mention here that for the majority of the threateners we look at--the authors of these threats--it appears that the message is not being used as a vehicle of communication, but rather is the "event" itself. As concerns the Secret Service, that raises a question: Does the assassin population come from a different group than the population of threateners?

There are some similarities between our problems and those of the Secret Service, especially as concerns methodology. For instance, we, too, are dealing with a low base rate phenomenon. Out of all the threats we have looked at, we have judged only two as having credibility. These two did not involve nuclear bombs. One was a non-nuclear threat. The other involved a threat to disperse radioactive material. In fact, a person was apprehended, and did have the stuff in his possession.

One important difference between our assessment and that of the Secret Service is that ours involves a rather elaborate evaluation process. There are different teams involved in different parts of the country, all linked by computer, and each team has a fairly broad variety of people in it. We do it very few times. We are talking about 50 or 60 of these nuclear events in the last 10 years. In contrast, the Secret Service has 20 or 30 investigations opened per day. And we are dealing primarily with written threats and have no opportunity to interview the threateners. That is because the author of the message rarely identifies himself--at least not directly--so that one could communicate with him further.

# COPING WITH VIOLENCE

W. Walter Menninger, M.D.
Senior Staff Psychiatrist
Division of Law and Psychiatry
Menninger Foundation
Topeka, Kansas

I.     Behavior of the Protected and Situations of Risk

In this conference, we are addressing a specific kind of potential violence:  assassination.  Management techniques may, therefore, be directed toward modifying any of the key elements which are necessary for an assassination to occur.  As noted by Shah[1], the key elements or variables are the targets (protected persons), settings and situations, and assailants (potential assassins).  While most of my remarks will address certain features of the assailants, I want to briefly touch some factors that should be considered with regard to the protected.

Noting that some victims of aggression, violence, and accidents have unconsciously played a part in eliciting that violence, Rothstein[2] has speculated about the unconscious factors in the psychology of those who become presidents or great leaders which might make them more prone to assassination.  In his review of the behavior of some of these leaders, Rothstein found some indications in their observable behavior of what one might view as unconscious fantasies of omnipotence or counterphobic elements aimed at mastering man's mortality.  As he puts it, "In one way, this could be viewed as evidence of an unrealistic belief in their own indestructibility which would allow them to take unwarranted risks."  However, he goes on to acknowledge:

> It appears that a successful leader may have
> to be an individual who acts as if he is, and perhaps
> in some ways believes himself to be, incapable of
> failure, assured of success.  This assuredness of
> success may have to be communicated to the public
> non-verbally by confident action.  Thus, the same
> attitude which conveys confidence to the public may
> make safety more difficult.[3]

The implications of these observations by Rothstein are that protected persons need to be confronted with what they are doing when they present a pattern of repeated risk-taking behavior.

With regard to excessive risk, the National Commission on the Causes and Prevention of Violence (1969) urged limiting the public

147

exposure of the president and presidential candidates and avoiding situations and settings which might increase the possibility of assassination. In its Final Report the Commission observed:

> There can be no perfect system for guarding the President short of isolating him, confining him to the White House and limiting his communication with the American public to television broadcasts and other media. This extreme solution is neither practicable nor desirable. For political reasons and for the sake of ceremonial traditions of the office, the American people expect the President to get out and "mingle with the people." (Among the eight [now ten] Presidents who have been assassination targets, all but Garfield and Truman were engaged in either ceremonial or political activities when they were attacked.) Still, a President can minimize the risk by carefully choosing speaking opportunities, public appearances, his means of travel to engagements, and the extent to which he gives advance notice of his movements. He can limit his public appearances to meeting places to which access is carefully controlled, especially by the use of electronic arms-detection equipment. Effective security can exist if a President permits.[4]

In order to achieve this reduction of risk, an effective alliance must be developed between the Secret Service and those it protects. In the case of the president, this means not only with the president himself, but with members of the president's family and key members of the presidential staff whose opinions can influence the president's behavior.

II. Factors in the Individual Which Contribute to Violence/ Assassination

Before discussing principles of management of potential assailants, it is well to review factors which underlie or precipitate violent action. While understanding these factors may not be critical in order to deal with an acutely violent situation, understanding is important if one seeks to prevent violence from occurring.

Violent behavior is commonly the end product of extreme anger (rage) or fear (panic), stemming from an actual or threatened injury or loss, which may be real or perceived. In assassination, the violence is directed toward a specific target--a significant governing leader who takes on a special symbolic meaning in the mind of the assailant. The motivating forces are usually multiple and both conscious--such as achieving political change or personal revenge--and unconscious--seeking to destroy a hurtful father figure and at the same time achieving unique recognition or martyrdom.

From his research of the violent interaction between individuals and authority figures (police officers), Toch made these observations about motives which underlie violent behavior:

> Our assumption is that if we want to explain why men are driven to acts of destruction, we must examine these acts, and we must understand the context in which they occur. We must know how destructive acts are initiated and developed, how they are conceived and perceived, and how they fit into the lives of their perpetrators.

> We must also assume that we cannot make sense of violent acts by viewing them as outsiders. Ultimately, violence arises because some person feels that he must resort to a physical act, that a problem he faces calls for a destructive solution. The problem a violent person perceives is rarely the situation as we see it, but rather some dilemma he feels he finds himself in. In order to understand a violent person's motives for violence, we must thus step into his shoes, and we must reconstruct his unique perspective, no matter how odd or strange it may be. We must recreate the world of the Violent Man, with all its fears and apprehensions, with its hopes and ambitions, with its strains and stresses.[5]

An additional perspective which may enhance the capacity to understand and deal with violent behavior is offered by Pinderhughes[6] from his work with violent marital situations. He calls attention to the frequency with which ambivalent motives are associated with violence. Also he notes that it is not possible to do violence without projecting evil onto the person who is the object of violence. This occurs through a paranoid process whereby that person represents a renounced and projected part of the self which is perceived as totally evil. Then, at the moment of violence, that person is viewed as an enemy who is deserving of destruction.

In the study of violent behavior in both clinical and non-clinical settings, various factors have been identified as predisposing, potentiating, and precipitating violent behavior. Some of the predisposing factors in the individual include a defect in the capacity for basic trust in relationships with others; exposure to violence in formative years by child abuse and family abuse; impaired ability to cope with frustration and anger through learning disability, mental retardation, or organic brain damage; and a defective sense of personal identity, self-esteem and self-integrity.

A number of environmental factors have been observed to increase the potential for aggressive behavior. As noted by O'Neal and McDonald[7], these are noise, heat, anonymity, diffusion of responsibility, audience approval, territoriality and crowding. With particular reference to an aspect of territoriality, Kinzel[8] discovered a significant difference in the "body buffer zone" of violent offenders, in contrast to non-violent offenders. This zone is the area surrounding the individual within which anxiety is produced if another person enters. Kinzel found the average body buffer zones of the violent group were almost four times larger than the zones for the non-violent group, particularly in the rear of the individual. He concluded that the violent offenders appeared to be most threatened by emotional and physical closeness, and that this sensitivity was rooted in problems dating back to pre-adolescent years. In many of his offenders there was evidence of homosexual panic.

The actual precipitation of violence is often triggered by a specific incident or an accumulation of stresses which prompts in the individual a feeling of desperation and a need to communicate that desperation or resolve the tension by violent action. At the point at which violence occurs, Toch[9] notes the intersection of three factors in the individual. First, there is an assumption that the authority has acted unfairly. Second, the individual concludes that the unfairness has reached a point where it cannot be further tolerated. Finally, the individual must feel a sufficient sense of potency (or disregard of consequence) to initiate violence.

With regard to the specific violence of assassination, Abrahamsen[10] and Rothstein[11,12] in testimony before the hearings on assassination and political violence, held by the National Commission on the Causes and Prevention of Violence, identified several characteristics of the potential assassin. Such a person commonly is more concerned about world events than his peers; he has exaggerated feelings of omnipotence, feeling he can do more to save the world than others; he is attention-seeking; and he often has significant resentment consciously felt toward the government for alleged mistreatment, either experienced personally or by persons or causes with which he deeply identifies and for which he feels a need for revenge.

III. Some Techniques for Managing Potentially Violent Persons

The management of the potential assassin by the Secret Service involves some direct activities--contact for assessment and surveillance--and some indirect activities--referral of individuals to appropriate community agencies (either police or mental health) for the institution of external control and possible treatment.

Clinically, violent persons may present any of several diagnostic pictures--paranoid, manic, antisocial, episodic dyscontrol, and so forth. Nevertheless, the experience of clinicians who have worked with violent persons suggests a number of principles to be considered in the direct contact with a potentially violent person. Most of these principles follow from an understanding of the psychology of the paranoid process and a sensitivity to approaches which respect the limited coping skills of the potentially violent person.

Some of the elements of interviewing have already been reviewed by Frazier and colleagues.[13] This subject is also discussed in a number of papers in the literature. Di Bella[14] outlines three steps in educating staff to manage threatening paranoid persons. He feels the first step is helping the staff appreciate the diagnostic features of a hostile, paranoid person. Second, he emphasizes the awareness and mastery of one's own feelings when one is dealing with a paranoid person. While Di Bella directs his attention toward persons working in a clinical setting, the principles he outlines are no less applicable in a non-clinical operation. The objective is to be sensitive to feelings generated in oneself during an interaction with a threatening, paranoid person, and to be able to use these feelings both diagnostically and, in a general sense, therapeutically. The third step suggested by Di Bella addresses the practical techniques:

> The [intervenor] must take a scrupulously
> frank, honest, straightforward and structured approach
> to the threatening [person]. He or she must not be
> too warm and friendly, or attempt to get close
> quickly. Touching . . . must be curtailed.
> Similarly, staff . . . should not approach the
> paranoid (person) suddenly and rapidly . . . .[15]

Since the paranoid person tends to project responsibility for problems elsewhere, he or she will not often seek help and initiative will have to be taken in offering resources to that person. The family should be engaged as much as possible in the process. Since the paranoid person usually explodes after the period of mounting tension, the intervenor needs to be alert to evidence of that tension or turmoil.

With regard to specific interventions, it is important to gauge the degree of failing psychic function on the part of the potential assailant and to arrange for intervention which will provide control, either physically or chemically. This may be through arranging referral for medication to reduce tension and activity, soliciting companionship by a significant person in the individual's life, or

151

arranging for protective custody in a hospital or detention facility. Where there is clear evidence of problems in judgment, it may be possible to refer the person to a setting where he can think and talk about his problems or concerns, and correct distorted perceptions and ideas by confrontation with the reality of the situation. If there appear to be some clear environmental factors contributing to the immediate crisis, it may be necessary to involve social work assistance or participation of a community agency that can attempt to alter the environmental stress.[16]

How can one change violent persons? Pinderhughes points out, "To change primitive thinking patterns, primitive methods are needed. When thinking patterns are unresponsibe to reason, pleasure or pain—in the form of reward or power—is required to change them."[17] In his discussion of strategies for changing violent persons, Toch believes that the task is to reduce the needs and incentives for the violent behavior, or to furnish alternative expressions or courses of action. He notes that violence is more likely to occur in men "who are unsure of their status or identity," and preventing violence requires an awareness and sensitivity to that. In instances where the Secret Service identifies a person in whom they feel an emotional illness is a significant factor, they need to have access to mental health resources to which they can refer such persons. These agencies may then apply medical/psychiatric approaches to the evaluation and treatment of the potentially violent person.[18,19]

IV. Special Considerations for Law Enforcement Officials

As noted previously, the potential for violent action may be potentiated by the way with which a potentially violent person is dealt. With particular reference to the role of law enforcement personnel in their contact with potentially violent people, Toch observes that "police officers sometimes unwittingly cooperate with self-defined champions by letting them play the role and crowding them into a duel." That is, the law enforcement officer may, by the way he approaches and deals with a potentially violent person, significantly potentiate and provoke a violent outcome.

Further, the potential for violence may be influenced by those persons who gravitate to the law enforcement profession to satisfy unconscious wishes to express violent impulses as well as to reinforce inner controls for those impulses. Drawing on his work with police officers, Toch made these observations:

> Our research indicates that the ranks of law
> enforcement contain their share of Violent Men. The
> personalities, outlooks and actions of these officers
> are similar to those of the other men in our sample. They
> reflect the same fears and insecurities, the same fragile,
> self-centered perspectives. They display the same bluster

and bluff, panic and punitiveness, rancor and revenge as do our other respondents. To be sure, the destructiveness of these officers is circumscribed by social pressure and administrative rules; but it is also protected by a code of mutual support and strong esprit de corps. And whereas much police violence springs out of adaptations to police work rather than out of problems of infancy, the result, in practice, is almost the same.[20]

One may assume that the Secret Service selection processes are much more rigorous than those of the police departments studies by Toch. Nonetheless, the training of Secret Service agents should be addressed to the potential errors that can be made in the interaction with a potentially violent person which increase the likelihood of a violent outcome.

## Notes

1. S. A. Shah, "Problems in Assessing and Managing Dangerous Behavior: Some Comments and Reflections," paper prepared for the Workshop on Behavioral Research and the Secret Service: Problems in Assessing and Managing Dangerous Behavior, Washington, D. C., March 1981.

2. D. A. Rothstein, "The Assassin and the Assassinated--as Non-patient Subjects of Psychiatric Investigation," in Dynamics of Violence, ed. J. Fawcett (Chicago: American Medical Association, 1971), pp. 145-55.

3. Ibid., p. 152.

4. M. Eisenhower et al., To Establish Justice, To Insure Domestic Tranquility, Final Report of the National Commission on the Causes and Prevention of Violence (Washington, D. C.: Government Printing Office, 1969), p. 131.

5. H. H. Toch, Violent Men (Chicago: Aldine, 1969), p. 5.

6. C. A. Pinderhughes, "Managing Paranoia in Violent Relationships," in Perspectives on Violence, ed. G. Usdin (New York: Brunner/Mazel, 1972), pp. 111-39.

7. E. C. O'Neal and P. J. McDonald, "The Environmental Psychology of Aggression, " in Perspectives on Aggression, eds. R. G. Geen and E. C. O'Neal (New York: Academic Press, 1976), pp. 169-92.

8. A. F. Kinzel, "Violent Behavior in Prisons," in Dynamics of Violence, ed. J. Fawcett (Chicago: American Medical Association, 1971), pp. 157-64.

9. Toch, <u>Violent Men</u>, p. 49.

10. D. Abrahamsen, Testimony at Hearing of the National Commission on the Causes and Prevention of Violence, Washington, D. C., October 3, 1968.

11. D. A. Rothstein, Testimony at Hearing of the National Commission on the Causes and Prevention of Violence, Washington, D. C., October 3, 1968.

12. D. A. Rothstein, "Presidential Assassination Syndrome," <u>Archives of General Psychiatry</u> 11 (September 1964): 245-54.

13. S. H. Frazier and colleagues, "Problems in Assessing and Managing Dangerous Behavior, paper prepared for the Workshop on Behavioral Research and the Secret Service: Problems in Assessing and Managing Dangerous Behavior, Washington, D. C., March 1981. Note especially "Conducting the Interview."

14. G. A. W. Di Bella, "Educating Staff to Manage Threatening Paranoid Patients," <u>American Journal of Psychiatry</u> 136 (March 1979): 333-35.

15. Ibid., p. 334.

16. R. W. Menninger and H. C. Modlin, "Individual Violence: Prevention in the Violence Threatening Patient, " in <u>Dynamics of Violence</u>, ed. J. Fawcett (Chicago: American Medical Association, 1971), pp. 71-78.

17. Pinderhughes, "Managing Paranoia in Violent Relationships," p. 123.

18. S. E. Edelman, "Managing the Violent Patient in a Community Mental Health Center," <u>Hospital and Community Psychiatry</u> 29 (July 1978): 460-62.

19. J. R. Lion, <u>Evaluation and Management of the Violent Patient</u> (Springfield, Ill.: C. C. Thomas, 1972).

20. Toch, <u>Violent Men</u>, p. 240.

# THE SECRET SERVICE AND THE MENTAL HEALTH DELIVERY SYSTEM: PROBLEMS AND PROSPECTS

Joseph T. English, M.D.
Director of Psychiatry
St. Vincent's Hospital
New York, New York

First, let me say a word about how we became involved in assisting the Secret Service in connection with the 1980 Democratic National Convention. Over a period of time, one of the St. Vincent resident psychiatrists had two patients that were a matter of concern to the Secret Service, one who was potentially threatening to Pope John Paul, II, when he was visiting New York and another who was threatening Senator Kennedy. The psychiatrist worked with a Secret Service agent who came to look into the situation. We were enormously impressed with the professionalism with which we were approached. As a result of our contact with these two patients, the location of St. Vincent's on the Lower West Side of Manhattan, and the fact that for the last two Democratic conventions St. Vincent's has been the medical back-up and has had a medical installation on the convention floor, we were asked if we would be willing to assist the Secret Service. We also learned that the Secret Service field headquarters happens to be in our cachment area.

Let me also share a personal experience that has influenced my response to the Secret Service request. Walter Menninger and I were working with the Peace Corps in Washington when the assassination of John F. Kennedy occurred in Dallas. I had the unfortunate experience of having to tell two immediate members of President Kennedy's family as to what had been learned in the Dallas emergency room. Subsequently, I spent four days in the White House helping Mr. Shriver to organize the funeral arrangements. During that period of time, one had a sense of the enormous impact of an event like this, not just on the people who came from all over the world, but as evidenced by the largest assemblage of heads of state in the history of the world attending the funeral. I had a chance to talk to some of the Secret Service agents, and it was very clear that they too were profoundly affected. Physicians have all had the experience of "losing" a patient and are trained to expect that as a part of their professional life. When the Secret Service loses a president, it is just as tough on them. I think the memory we all have of such events affects our willingness to help the Secret Service.

However, not all my colleagues were sympathetic.

In a department like ours, we discuss this sort of thing before we get into it, and despite my mind set, a good many thorny issues

155

were raised. First, there were the legal issues, the ethical issues, the confidentiality issues, and the liability issues that hospitals worry about these days. Second, there were questions as to just what we had to offer the Secret Service, recognizing the limitations of our predictive ability. We had long discussions about these questions. Third, someone raised the concern: "What is this going to do to the image of our department? We will be considered the Lower West Side extention of the Gulag Archipelago; the Secret Service today and the FBI and the CIA tomorrow." Someone else said, "Listen, we are trying to provide treatment here. What is the effect of this involvement going to be on our patient care environment?" Yet another colleague queried, "Where are we going to get the financial support? Are these patients going to be covered, and how long are we going to have them after the Secret Service and the convention leave town? We know you are trying to kill the president, but do you have Blue Cross?" Finally, I think we were concerned that we might somehow raise some false expectations about what we could do in relationship to this enormous responsibility that the Secret Service was going to take on.

Despite all of that we said, yes, we would do it. Somewhat in the Peace Corps spirit, we decided if we were going to do it, we would avoid the way mental health professionals often do these things, i.e., in total isolation and without any sense of the context of what the Secret Service is up against.

We met with the agents that were going to be involved in this task on their turf, in their headquarters. In their conference room, we met a bright, interesting and obviously concerned group of agents. I took our clinical director, our chief resident, and some of the others who would actually be involved at St. Vincent's. The first thing our clinical director did was to get up and say, "Look, what worries us most is that we are going to create expectations just by being here that we cannot fulfill. We are going to start by telling you what we cannot do." He proceeded to explain the commitment laws of the State of New York, the fact that we could not be involved in preventive detention, that essentially where we could help was if someone was clearly mentally ill and in our judgment represented a danger to himself or someone else. We tried to give a feel for what the ground rules are in our world, the world of the psychiatric hospital in New York City.

It became apparent that something we could do would be to expedite the evaluation of people that the Secret Service agents would want to have evaluated. It became obvious in the discussion that one of their problems is it can take a lot of time to get an evaluation done in a large medical center. Setting up arrangements that would provide a fast-track evaluation would be useful to limit the time agents would be away from their primary area of activity, i.e., the convention.

When we met in advance with the Secret Service, we arranged to have a debriefing, within one week or two after the convention, to see what we might have learned together. By that time, we had also received word from David Hamburg about this meeting, and we said, "Perhaps there will be something coming out of the convention collaboration that might be relevant to a meeting such as this." I must say they were as enthusiastic about that as we were.

Our actual experience was really anticlimactic. We were asked to evaluate only two patients who were brought to the emergency room. One we hospitalized, clearly mentally ill, a chronic paranoid schizophrenic who was up in the Waldorf looking for Senator Kennedy who "owed him a lot of money"; he himself was "a billionaire," had "23 Nobel prizes", and all the rest, and was very angry about all this money that Senator Kennedy owed him.

When he came to the emergency room, the question of mental illness was clear, but the dangerousness determination was made by the clinical director together with our resident's perception of the agents' expertise in this regard. The agents' judgment was that this person was imminently dangerous and their opinion was a critical factor in influencing that admission.

In the other instance, there was evidence of a personality disorder, but certainly no major mental illness requiring treatment, no interest in treatment; and the person was discharged.

From our experience, let me offer several observations. First, it was enormously important to have the prior association to the event that was developed between our hospital and the Secret Service itself. We wonder whether every field station of the Secret Service--certainly in major cities where protected persons are coming in and out--might not establish such a relationship, develop rapport and mutual understanding so that whatever help a medical center could give could be facilitated.

Second, though we got a clear perception of what the agents' task was, it was very clear that they had great compassion for some of these people that they would see who might or might not be dangerous but who clearly were in need of help from some mental health professional. It was obvious that what we were able to offer was helpful, i.e., some evaluation and an attempt to link that person to some kind of mental health care which would not only be good for the individual but, hopefully, would also reduce the possibility of what the Secret Service is principally concerned with preventing. The issue of training fascinated us as well. After our initial meeting with the agents before the convention, they started asking us about how they could improve their ability to assess dangerousness. However, sitting there with them, we developed enormous respect for their experience and expertise in this regard. To be quite frank, we

157

were very worried about contaminating that expertise, so we said, "We have nothing at this point to say to you in that regard. We really wonder about our own profession's ability. We would suggest that you continue doing whatever you have done. At some point we may have something to contribute. Right now, when you think mental illness is a major factor and you are wondering about its impact on the problem with which you are concerned, we will be glad to be a part of the picture; but you may be much more adept at this than we are." We think that statement may have reinforced whatever sense of adequacy they had and maybe that was, in itself, valuable. Our concern about the training issue would come down to this: On the basis of the discussions that we have had with them, it is clear that they are supporting a lot of chronic schizophrenics, but we don't think they do this essentially to perform a mental health function. We think that is another way they have of getting the kinds of information that they need to do their job, and I cannot think of a way that we could more misserve them than to try to turn them into amateur mental health professionals. We would, however, like to experiment with ways in which we could reinforce each other's adequacies in dealing with problems of great mutual interest.

# LEGAL AND ETHICAL IMPLICATIONS OF SECRET SERVICE INTERVENTION

Charles R. Halpern, J.D.
Associate Professor and Director
Institute for Public Representation
Georgetown University Law Center
Washington, D. C.

In general, I will limit my comments to what we might call involuntary or unwelcome intervention. If the Secret Service adopts as a strategy getting a dangerous person out of Los Angeles by sending him to Hawaii for a couple of weeks while the president is visiting, that is the kind of intervention that I think does not pose legal or ethical problems, but as the discussion last night and today has suggested, intervention can sometimes come in less benign guises. It can involve triggering a civil commitment process. It can involve a more or less intrusive kind of surveillance which might involve interviews or discussions with the employer of the person or members of his family or circle. Those kinds of interventions could have extremely negative consequences for the person who is the subject of those interventions.

I should think that being identified by the Secret Service as a threat to the president or another protected person could have really quite devastating effects on the life of the person into whose world this intervention comes. An argument for humility in intervention grows out of the statistics that John Monahan gave us--that mental health professionals have, at best, a one-in-three success rate in predicting dangerous behavior. Nothing I have heard today suggests that the present prediction rate of the Secret Service would be any higher than that now or in the foreseeable future.

In thinking about the legal and ethical implications of intervention, it is appropriate to take a moment to step back and look at some of the other values and legal considerations that are implicated when such an intervention is made.

First and foremost there is the presumption of innocence. We are, as American citizens, presumed innocent until proven guilty. By hypothesis, most of the interventions will be into the lives of citizens who have committed no crime and been convicted of no crime. It is true some of them may have violated the threat statute, but they have not been adjudicated in any event. Many others have not even arguably committed any crime. So there is that highly prized, constitutionally-based value that must be taken into account.

159

Second, there is what might be called the right to privacy or, more generically, the right to be left alone. We all have the right to be left alone unless we commit an act which has been defined as criminal. As for the mentally ill or arguably mentally ill suspect, each state has a commitment law which defines mental illness and defines what kinds of consequences can flow from that characterization.

In thinking about Secret Service intervention, it is important to consider not only the mandate of the Service to protect the person of the president and certain other enumerated people, but also to consider the structure of constitutional principles and laws which limit the Secret Service as well as all other policing agencies.

It is important to remember that, as special as the Secret Service mandate is, it is not unique. The Federal Bureau of Investigation, for example, has responsibilities which are no less awesome than those of the Secret Service. Ted Kennedy, after all, is protected one day by the Secret Service and the next day by the FBI. Nancy Reagan is a protected by the Secret Service, but the problems of protecting her are probably no more awesome than the problems of guarding against the kind of nuclear disaster that Brian Jenkins was discussing this morning.

So, it is important to think sympathetically and constructively about the Secret Service's situation, but not to make the mistake of thinking that this is some kind of unique problem in the world of American policing that is discontinuous from all other problems of that dimension. This should be a cautionary note, if we start thinking about amending federal laws to help deal with threats to protected persons. The "protected" category is an arbitrarily defined creature of a couple of legislative spasms. It does not define the category of those in greatest jeopardy or those whom our country can least afford to lose.

Moving on to the subject of the interface between the mental health professionals and the Secret Service, I think many of the suggestions that came up in my workshop group and that I have heard in the plenary make a great deal of sense for facilitating an effective relationship; but again, my suggestion is that psychiatrists and other mental health professionals should not "throw away the book" when it comes to dealing with the Secret Service and the persons it protects.

Many of you are probably familiar with the Tarasoff decision in California about the obligations of a psychiatrist when one of his

160

patients makes a credible threat against another person.*  That seems to me to be the appropriate kind of analysis for mental health professionals to make in deciding what their obligations to their patients are, how the confidentiality obligation should be interpreted, and the like.  The fact that a patient threatens Senator Kennedy <u>before</u> he withdraws from the presidential race rather than <u>afterwards</u>, which is the litmus paper test for Secret Service protection, does not resolve the question for the therapist of when to break confidentiality.

This leads me to the conclusion, at least until I am persuaded otherwise, that there is no need for special federal commitment legislation or other legislation to deal with those who threaten persons protected by the Secret Service.  A better assessment of state laws, smoother coordination, and anticipatory coordination between the Secret Service and state facilities all seem quite appropriate, but I do not believe that this is a situation in which special laws should be contemplated or passed.

Finally, let me just note that the problem of intervention is much larger than the interface between mental health problems and the Secret Service mandate, which has tended to dominate our discussion today.  A significant number of people who are of concern to the Secret Service are not even arguably mentally ill.  The Puerto Rican nationalists who shot up the House of Representatives were not, to the best of my knowledge, even arguably mentally ill.  James Earl Ray was not arguably mentally ill.  I understand that some significant number of the 300 "Quarterly Investigation" subjects are not even arguably mentally ill.  The problem with intervention in that situation is still more acute.  We do, at least, have some laws and some intellectual constructs for justifying intervention to prevent dangerous behavior by people who are arguably mentally ill; but if one is talking about people who are not, then from the standpoint of law and ethics one has an even more complicated problem.

We have not yet gotten into the question of the intervention strategies that the Secret Service uses in those contexts.  It would perhaps be an interesting subject for inquiry, and from the legal standpoint an even more difficult one.

Let me end by expressing my sympathy for the enormous task that falls to the Secret Service and my gratitude to these people who seem to discharge this responsibility with so much sensitivity and so much loyalty to their duties.

---

*Tarasoff v. Regents of the University of California, 529 P.2d 553 (Cal. 1974), vac., reheard in bank, and aff'd. 551 P.2d 334 (Cal. 1976).

I think, however, that there are legal and constitutional limitations as to what kinds of interventions are justifiable to control the behavior of dangerous people. They are not matters of legal technicality or changing a particular test in a jurisdiction to the left or to the right. They are fundamental questions about how we have ordered our affairs as a society. This leads me back to the point that Dave Hamburg has raised in this conference, namely to think about other ways in which we can facilitate the Secret Service in the discharge of its responsibilites through altering the behavior of protected persons.

# ETHICAL AND MEDICAL IMPLICATIONS OF SECRET SERVICE INTERVENTION

Robert Michels, M.D.
Barklee McKee Professor of Psychiatry
Cornell University Medical College
Psychiatrist-in-Chief
The New York Hospital
New York, New York

One of the themes of the afternoon has been the potentially different ethical standards which we might apply to the behavior of different classes of persons. For example, consider citizens in general. The ethical standards are those that would apply to a used car dealer or soap salesman. Government agents might be different. I can imagine things that one might find acceptable in a private citizen, but not acceptable in a government agent. Finally, a member of a profession might be judged by still a third set of standards. There might be knowledge that we would consider appropriate for a government agent to use, but not appropriate for a professional to reveal.

We must consider the difference between these roles and, also, the significance of the blurring among them that might occur with certain types of arrangements between the government and the professions. The word "co-opt" was used earlier, and some might even say that everyone in this room has been co-opted.

Shifting to another issue, we are talking about a population of persons at least a significant portion of whom demonstrate behaviors that would suggest that mental health professionals might have relevant expertise regarding their management. However, these persons are not identified as patients and do not have doctor-patient or caretaker-patient relationships with mental health professionals. We are asking, "What are the rules under those circumstances?" The answer is that we do not have clear rules under those circumstances, and we tend to get into difficulty as a result.

There are two different conflicts that we have been discussing. One involves conflicting values that are respected by the Service. The mission of the Secret Service is to protect its "protectees." At the same time, like everyone else in our society, Secret Service personnel recogize and are constrained by the rights of citizens, and they have to deal with the tensions between the mission and those rights. We heard in the case presentations last night how they have to balance these two values.

A third value that is clearly lower in priority, but recurrent in the discussion, is the desire of Secret Service agents to help people in need. It is not part of their official mission, nor is being helped by the Secret Service a right of the people whom they approach. Yet that theme emerges repeatedly. It is interesting in part because it may offer a way of resolving some of the conflicts between the first two values. It might be that the best way to guarantee the safety of protected persons, and at the same time to respect the rights of citizens in whom the Service becomes interested, is to assume a helping role--as exemplified, for instance, by sending a "dangerous" subject on vacation for the week that the president is in town.

The other tension that we have discussed is the tension between two basic frames of reference in ethical discourse, the consequentialist and the deontologic. As applied to the Secret Service, the former might refer to what would result if the Service followed a certain course of action, while the latter would involve consideration of what basic principles of human value should determine how the Service is to function.

This came up clearly in one of the cases presented last night, in which we heard the tension between the official justification for an act which included concern for the basic rights of the subject, and the more urgent consequential analysis in the statement, "We got the gun away from him but I am not sure I want to tell you how." This is an inevitable tension in front line work, whether it be in a psychiatric emergency room where there is a document to be signed that says "voluntary consent for admission" (but we often prefer not to know how the signature got there), or in a police station where a subject negociates with an officer concerning whether he can go home or must spend the night in the station. One of the dangers in this kind of tension between avowed principles and immediate consequences is that it creates the possibility of a crisis if it should become clear that the principle was violated in practice, with a backlash that can have very dramatic consequences.

Some problems are related to the types of interventions that are used. Charles Halpern has emphasized that the very act of investigating involves potential intrusions into privacy, a value held dearly in our society. In addition, at times there is deceit, or at least the failure to disclose the person's individual rights to him. For example, it was not clear that the two persons who were brought by Secret Service agents to St. Vincent's Hospital [New York City] were told that they had no obligation to go there.[1] We heard the examining physician say that he returned the patient to the

---

*See presentation by Joseph English, page 155.

164

"custody" of the agent, although the agent never had custody in the first place. The physician's confusion would certainly raise questions concerning whether the patient knew that he was not in custody. Still other problems arise in response to the use of overt coercion.

Finally, the least noxious type of intervention leads to the most interesting problems: the dependency that develops in response to long-term supportive contact. For example, in one of the cases we learned about, the Secret Service may have become the most meaningful relationship in the subject's life. There is an old Chinese custom that if you save a man's life you are responsible to care for him forever. One might argue that the Secret Service develops a caretaking responsibility as a result of its intervention because it becomes the next of kin to some of its subjects.

One way of solving some of these problems is to provide attractive interventions rather than noxious ones, so that subjects will embrace the interventions rather than shrink from them. For subjects who are mentally ill, facilitating good treatment might be a socially acceptable, attractive, and effective strategy for diminishing risks without infringing on rights.

Charles Halpern says that he does not think that we should change our medical ethics because the person being threatened is or is not protected by the Secret Service. I agree, but the Service may want to change medical decisions rather than medical ethics. You can change decisions without changing principles by using the Service's resources to change the cost/benefit ratio of different courses of action. For example, if the Service made treatment resources available for subjects, those treatments might be prescribed more often by those caring for them, and if those treatments happened to contribute to the safety of the Service's protected persons, that might be to everyone's benefit.

Most of the intervention strategies we have heard discussed have been acute strategies. Most of the psychopathology we have heard described has been chronic psychopathology. The current health delivery system in psychiatry does not provide adequate chronic care for most patients. Instead, what the Secret Service can expect from the mental health care system is a series of acute interventions for people with chronic diseases who have as a recurring symptom threats to protected persons. This is not a rational treatment strategy; it simply reflects the general irrationality of the treatment offered the chronically mentally ill. If the Service is going to offer rational intervention systems, it will have to build its own because no others are available. This would be a formidable task, but it might be the cheapest, most humane, and most libertarian way to manage 300 subjects who cause the greatest concern.

# PERSONAL LIBERTY AND THE SECRET SERVICE PROTECTIVE FUNCTION

Charles H. Whitebread, L. L. B.
Visiting Professor of Law
University of Southern California Law Center
Los Angeles, California

I concur with Charles Halpern that no issue has for so long tested our legal system as devising lawful means in our free society for preventing criminality. We are correctly skeptical of restraining liberty unless that restraint is based upon demonstrable conduct. Removing people from the streets--putting them in even temporary restraint--on mere hints and suspicions, will not square with the constitutional ideal. Of course, part of our concern stems from lack of confidence in the dangerousness assessment, but even if we were far more sure of our predictions than the present state of the art in behavioral science permits, I would not condone or advocate restriction of constitutional liberty interests of citizens without demonstrable anti-social conduct.

This preference for liberty and personal privacy has certainly made law enforcement in general and the Secret Service protective function in particular more difficult. In other countries the counterparts of the Secret Service can sweep the streets clear without the need even for reasonable suspicion. We have made the social policy judgment that such police conduct may damage society more than the harm it seeks to prevent.

This choice of a free society in favor of personal liberty has made the job of the Secret Service more difficult, but there are at least three concepts of constitutional criminal procedure which may serve to help the Service in fulfilling its mission. First, there is a significant line of cases permitting police officials to stop and briefly detain any citizen reasonably suspected of involvement in crime. So long as the officer's suspicion is reasonable and articulable, detention is authorized even if no crime has been committed. Officers may detain for investigation those they reasonably suspect may commit crimes. These short-term investigative detentions on the standard of reasonable suspicion provide law enforcement officers a significant weapon in the crime prevention effort.

Second, as some of the Secret Service representatives pointed out in the planning session for this conference, the Secret Service surveillance and investigation may in itself have deterrent value. For example, if the agent investigating Mr. Smith during a visit by a protected person to Smith's town says, "During the visit, I will be assigned to you. You can be sure I will be right with you all during this time," such surveillance deters. There may be some hypothetical legal cause of action by the person under surveillance, but so long as the decision to undertake the surveillance is reasonable, I suspect courts will err on the side of approving the investigative conduct, especially in light of the minimal nature of the intrusion compared to the significance of the Secret Service protective function.

Third, many state law provisions for emergency civil commitment may permit constitutional restraint of the acutely mentally ill at least for a period sufficient to permit the protected person to finish his visit and leave town. While we have heard of the inadequacy of some state mental health laws during this conference, I do not think amendment of federal law to permit easier commitment of those assessed dangerous is advisable. The Secret Service has an awesome responsibility to protect our leaders; nevertheless, that function is neither unique nor considerably more important than the duties of other police agencies such as the FBI, airport police, harbor patrol, customs and immigration authorities and the like. Tampering with legal bars to involuntary loss of liberty is dangerous. We must remember the fundamental principle that once any citizen's liberty is unfairly or unconstitutionally lost, even in the name of a noble cause, all of us have lost some part of our hard-won liberty.

This libertarian rhetoric, while not new, needs no apology as an appropriate restraint on hasty proposals for easing the way to involuntary losses of liberty.

As to the other legal issues--which often trail or precede moral and ethical questions as well--I concur in the view of the planning committee that they are best saved for full discussion at some later conference and are not best served with short shrift here.

# SOME THOUGHTS ON "THREATS" AND FREE SPEECH, AND CASE MANAGEMENT

R. Kirkland Gable, Ed.D., J.D.
Associate Professor
Department of Psychology
California Lutheran College
Thousand Oaks, California

I would like briefly to discuss some of the things that go into weighing competing interests. The Supreme Court in the Watts case[1], set out some issues in viewing 18 USC 871, the so-called "threat statute," with which we are in some measure concerned here today. The Court said that the statute under which the petitioner was convicted was constitutional on its face. The nation undoubtedly has a valid, even an overwhelming, interest in the protection of the safety of the Chief Executive, and in allowing him to perform his duties without interference or threats of physical violence. Nevertheless, a statute such as this one, which makes criminal a form of pure speech, must be interpreted with the commands of the First Amendment clearly in mind. What is a threat must be distinguished from what is constitutionally protected speech.

In these types of cases, there has been something of a separation between an absolute threat and a conditional threat. As an example of an absolute threat, let me cite an old case, Ragansky[2], in which the fellow said something like, "We ought to make the biggest bomb in the world and take it down to the White House and put it on the dome and blow up President Wilson and all the rest of the crooks." That is a kind of statement for which the fellow was convicted under the threat statute. In contrast, here is an example of a conditional threat, which looks like political hyperbole: "Now, I have already received my draft classification as A-1, and I have got to report for my physical this Monday. I am not going. If they ever make me carry a rifle, the first man I want to get in my sights is LBJ." If a statement is conditional, there is no conviction.

When we begin to look at the intent of the person, we balance the likelihood of particular risks. We are looking at the purpose of free speech, and so on. My guess is that there should perhaps be a

clarification of what is legally required for conviction and what is permissible. Such clarification might not involve changes in statutes, but rather issuance of guidelines as to what is permitted versus what constitutes a threat, and so on. There is, perhaps, something useful as a guideline in Tarasoff[3], regardless of how one may feel about that case.

169

Turning to an issue which was illustrated last night in the case presentations, I am wondering whether we might want to think about increasing the use of conditional release from hospitals for subjects we know are about to be discharged. Perhaps the release would be conditional upon medication maintenance of some kind, non-possession of certain kinds of weapons, or specified limitations in travel. We might begin by examining legally and clinically relevant conditions that might be placed on travel. The use of case managers to monitor such subjects upon their conditional release might be an appropriate strategy. I am inclined to mention a device used at one time by the late Dr. Schwitzgebel[4,5], who was a close friend of mine--an electronic monitoring system for tracking the locations of persons released from institutions. This equipment allowed the monitoring of a person every 30 seconds as he or she travelled in an urban area, and was required as a condition of release. The person was free at any time to return to the mental hospital or prison, if he or she so desired. (Very few wished to do that.) I think there are probably many such intervention strategies which could be devised and used effectively.

The issues are not going to be so clearly civil libertarian versus police. What we really need is a more thoughtful consideration of the legitimate competing interests and a clarification of what happens in practice--not what happens on paper and who signs admission certificates, and so on. We need a really serious and honest look at the processing of these people; and where critical legal issues are raised, we need to begin to develop guidelines for handling such persons.

### Notes

1. Watts v. United States, 394 U.S. 705 (1969).

2. Ragansky v. United States, 253 F. 643 (CA7, 1918).

3. Tarasoff v. Regents of the University of California, 529 P.2d 533 (Cal. 1974), vac., reheard in bank, and aff'd. 551 P.2d 334 (Cal. 1976).

4. R. Schwitzgebel, "Development of an Electronic Rehabilitation System for Parolees," Law and Computer Technology 2 (1969): 9-12.

5. Anthropotelemetry: Dr. Schwitzgebel's Machine, Harvard Law Review 80 (1966): 403-21.

MEMORANDUM

Research and Legal Issues

R. Kirkland Gable, Ed.D., J.D.
Associate Professor of Psychology
California Lutheran College
Thousand Oaks, California

(1)   It was indicated in a summary of the November 13, 1980, planning committee meeting that more than half the subjects the Secret Service deals with have mental health problems.  This seems to be an unusually high percentage.  Is is possible that the Service over-selects some persons because they have a mental history?  This could result in an unnecessarily high percentage of false positives. Professor Zimring's proposed research design using "proxy" behaviors could help to answer this question if subpopulations are sampled from persons with and without mental histories across categories of persons receiving various Service interventions.  (Incidentally, additional "proxy" behaviors might include aggressive driving behaviors or offenses, violent sports such as hunting, child abuse, sleep disturbance, and behaviors related to agitated depression.)

(2)   Some aggressive behaviors may be state-dependent.  They may occur primarily with the use of alcohol or prohibited drugs or in the absence of psychotropic medication.*  If this is so, then perhaps interviews and other assessment procedures might be conducted when the subjects are in these particular states of conciousness. Similarly, therapeutic intervention might be most effectively conducted in these altered states.  Finally, certain Secret Service surveillance, restraint, or other intervention procedures might be legally conditioned upon the subject's likely states of consciousness and medication compliance.

(3)   Assessment might involve some consideration of the extent to which the dangerous conduct is spontaneous (impulsive) or planned (instrumental) or a combination of these modes.  If the subject's aggressive target is narrow and specific, therapeutic intervention might involve stimulus narrowing and desensitization procedures.  If stress interviews appear to increase the probability of subsequent

---

*See V. I. Reus, H. Weingartner, and R. M. Post, "Clinical Implications of State-Dependent Learning," American Journal of Psychiatry 136 (1979):  927-31; and C. L. Cunningham, "Alcohol as a Cure for Extinction: State Dependency Produced by Conditioned Inhibition," Animal Learning and Behavior 7 (1979):  45-52.

171

dangerous behaviors, they might be followed by relaxation interviews conducted by clinicians to mitigate the effects of stress interviews. Some useful information might also be obtained from these interviews by assessing the extent to which a subject can remain relaxed in the presence of target stimuli that usually elicit aggressive responses.

(4) Although it is tempting to compromise the legal rights of subjects in balancing potential costs and benefits, caution should be exercised in this regard. Management and intervention strategies might be designed with the doctrine of "least restrictive alternatives" in mind. However, certain assumed "alternatives" may in fact be mere illusions of choice if they do not have empirically measurable consequences. Thus, the formulation of legal and policy recommendations should be sensitive to empirical findings in the difficult task of balancing competing, legitimate public and private interests.

## Some Thoughts Stimulated by the Conference

(1) There may be some value in more extensively using metal detection devices for screening persons in proximity to the President. This was mentioned at the conference.

(2) As a time-limited research project, persons in public crowds near the president might be randomly sampled and screened for possession of firearms, mental history, Secret Service investigative status, and so on. This would give researchers some impression as to the risk of public appearances of the president. It could also be used to assess the effectiveness of Secret Service interventions as shown by a reduced number of "problematic" persons in public crowds.

(3) Systematic or discretionary searches might be made of persons in proximity to the president without the usual legal standard of probable cause. Persons within a specified proximity to the president would be deemed to have given express or implied consent to a search. By analogy, implied consent is given for blood alcohol testing by the act of driving a motor vehicle in some jurisdictions. (Here we are dealing with equal or substantially greater risks presented by the illegal conduct of persons.) In addition, express consent could be obtained, if necessary, by making public announcement, both verbal and posted, prior to the president's arrival.

(4) Electronic monitoring equipment is readily available and has been used to record the location of mental patients and parolees as a method to protect the public. While the use of such equipment is not necessarily recommended, its capability is worth noting.

172

## Bibliography

Schwitzgebel, R. L., and Schwitzgebel, R. K.  Law and Psychological
Practice.  New York:  John Wiley and Sons, 1980.

MEMORANDUM

On Assessment

Kenneth R. Hammond, Ph.D.
Professor of Psychology
Center for Research on Judgment and Policy
University of Colorado
Boulder, Colorado


There has been considerable research on human judgment and
decision-making over the past 25 years. (Persons familiar with the
field estimate that the number of empirical papers published in
refereed journals exceeds 3,000 and may be as high as 5,000.) There
is, in short, an empirical research basis for the following
conclusions:

1. Judgments in general are highly fallible.
2. Fallibility increases as the "softness" of the judgment
task increases--that is, as the judgment becomes increasingly
intuition-dependent.
3. Predictions of behavior based on judgment are particularly
fallible.
4. Expert judgment regarding the prediction of behavior is
almost certainly no better than that of the nonexpert. (Clinical
judgment has been studied since the early 1950s; there is no evidence
whatever that clinical judgment of any kind is as good as actuarial
prediction, and considerable evidence that it is worse.)

These conclusions are as firmly based as any conclusions in the field
of behavioral science.

The empirical findings noted above, together with (a)
theoretical, analytical treatment of the prediction problem, and (b)
general descriptions of the situation faced by the Secret Service
agent in the field, and his consultants, lead to the conclusions:

1. These four findings indicated above are applicable to the
judgments that must be made by the agent in the field, and
2. to any mental health professional to whom he might turn
for consultation. Furthermore,
3. because of the agents' duty to intervene (that is, to
interview and occasionally restrain persons of interest), it will be
very difficult, and perhaps impossible, to carry out research aimed
at improving the predictive accuracy of the judgments that must be
made by the Secret Service agents and their consultants from the
mental health profession.

175

Recommendations:

    1. It will not be useful to recapitulate the experience of the past 25 years by carrying out new studies with Secret Service personnel. Such studies would be expensive, time-consuming for both researchers and Secret Service personnel, and have a very low probability of teaching us anything new. In the absence of highly compelling reasons to believe that Secret Service agents or their consultants possess some special abilities heretofore wholly unobserved in other professionals, research that merely recapitulates previous work cannot be justified; therefore it should not be undertaken. Retrospective analyses will almost certainly be worthless in view of the fact of intervention.

    2. The research that has been done on judgments, decision-making, and prediction of behavior suggests, but does not prove, that there is some value to be derived from decision support systems. In the case of the Secret Service, an effort to develop such a system might prove to be worthwhile, particularly if it were closely related to a management information system that was developed with research needs in mind. Such a system may decrease the work load of the agency by leading to improvements in

- the information system upon which the agency depends
- the retraceability of decisions
- the uniformity of the decision-making process
- the training of agents with regard to predictions of behavior.

MEMORANDUM

The Escalating Incidence of Assassination

Brian M. Jenkins
Director, Security and Subnational Conflict Program
Rand Corporation
Santa Monica, California

## 1.    Assassination:  A Growing Problem

Assassinations worldwide have increased.  The total volume of
terrorist activity increased during the 1968 to 1980 period, and
assassinations also increased as a percentage of all terrorist
incidents.  More than 500 assassinations occur annually worldwide.

Not only do we see an increase in assassinations by terrorist
groups, but government-backed assassination campaigns directed
against foreign or domestic foes abroad also have increased.  For
example, Libyan assassins are believed responsible for a number of
murders last year of Libyans living abroad who failed to heed Colonel
Qadaffi's warning to return.

The United States has not been immune to this crime.  Last
year, anti-Castro Cuban emigres assassinated a Cuban diplomat in New
York.  In 1976, anti-Castro extremists killed a former Chilean
cabinet minister in Washington at the behest of the Chilean secret
police.  In 1980, a gunman or gunmen, believed to be in the employ of
Iran, shot to death a former Iranian official in Washington.

## 2.    Rand's Research on Political Violence

Since 1972, the Rand Corporation has been engaged in research
on various aspects of political violence, terrorism and low-level
conflict.  This research effort has examined the origins and theory
of modern terrorism, the mindset and modus operandi of various
terrorist groups, the specific problem of political kidnappings, and
trends in terrorism.  None of these studies specifically addresses
evaluating threats to the president and other persons protected by
the U. S. Secret Service.  However, one current research project does
deal with the problem of assessing the credibility of threat messages
involving nuclear-related extortion.

## 3.    Rand's Threat Credibility Assessment Project

Since 1970, there have been approximately 50 threat messages in
which the author or authors threatened to detonate a nuclear

explosive device or disperse radioactive material in an American city. These events, although generally not publicized, create considerable disruption and could, if publicized, cause alarm and panic. Following such a threat in Los Angeles in 1975, it was deemed necessary to create a capability for rapidly assessing the credibility of nuclear threat messages.

Two developments are making the traditional method of assessing the credibility of nuclear threats more difficult. Although there is confidence in U. S. safeguards and accounting systems, there is an increasing amount of nuclear material beyond American control. The spread of nuclear programs throughout the world makes it increasingly difficult to say with a high degree of confidence that the authors of such a threat do not possess nuclear material.

The spread of nuclear knowledge increases the number of people who possess at least a theoretical knowledge of nuclear weapons design. Even a layman, with little technical background, can use the right words. It becomes more and more likely that the designs or equations submitted to support a nuclear threat will be correct. These developments place a growing burden on a behavioral assessment in support of the technical assessment. The development of a behavioral assessment capability is Rand's current task.

When a nuclear message is received by the FBI, which has jurisdiction over violations of the Atomic Energy Act, it is immediately forwarded to a special FBI desk in Washington. The Emergency Action Coordination Team in the Department of Energy is notified. This team then activates the Threat Assessment Team (TAT). The TAT consists of separate teams linked by computer but working separately, at least until after the initial assessment is made. The teams at Los Alamos and Lawrence Livermore laboratories address the technical and operational aspects of the message. Other teams address the behavioral aspects. The combined assessments are communicated to the Department of Energy.

The research and actual threat assessment experience thus far have demonstrated the feasibility and utility of a behavioral assessment capability. We are in the process of systematizing conclusions from research and lessons learned in evaluating threats into a list of credibility criteria. The behavioral assessment capability is being expanded to other areas.

While the Department of Energy's system for assessing nuclear threat messages is elaborate and involves teams including physicists, psychiatrists, psychologists, propaganda analysts, and persons with other specified skills, portions of this work may provide a model for developing a similar, although necessarily less elaborate, capability in support of Secret Service activities.

MEMORANDUM

Prediction Research

John Monahan, Ph.D.
Professor of Law and Professor of Psychology
University of Virginia Law School
Charlottesville, Virginia


I would offer four observations for consideration by workshop participants prior to our March 8 meeting.

(1) I strongly support the suggestion by Frank Zimring* for "proxy studies" of the validity of Secret Service predictions of violent behavior. Without the use of reasonable proxies for attempted assassination, I doubt that validation research in this area can ever be done due to the extremely low base rate of the criterion. Such a research strategy could have useful secondary benefits as well. If it were found that agents in the course of their work were relatively accurate at predicting violent behavior, but that the violence was usually directed at persons other than those the Service protects ("proxies"), implications for cooperation with local authorities might be forthcoming. For example, to the extent that the persons predicted to be violent were also believed to be mentally ill, referral to a local department of mental health for civil commitment may be advisable. While this would not further the specific goals of the Secret Service, it would, to the extent the predictions were accurate, result in a decrease of violence in society. This would be no small thing.

(2) There is reason to question the generalizability of the existing research on violence prediction to the concerns of the Secret Service. While agents certainly should be aware of the factors that seem to anticipate violence in other contexts, it is unknown to what extent those factors apply to the kinds of "political" violence of interest to the Secret Service. All of the research with which I am familiar deals with "street violence." Perhaps, as Frank's memorandum implies, only certain kinds of street violence are the functional equivalents of political violence. I raise this point because I am struck by the fact that one factor--race--that is always implicated in predictive accounts of street violence seems not at all implicated, or even implicated in the opposite direction, in political assassination. While blacks are highly overrepresented in street violence, all of the attempted presidential assassins I am aware of were white.

---

*Page 183.

(3) "Process studies" of the reliability of agent decision-making on predictive tasks may be of value. Given the difficulty of empirically studying the accuracy (validity) of agent predictions, perhaps one useful fall-back strategy would be to study the factors that lead agents to disagree on the extent to which the same persons are a threat. This was begun in the 1976 study by Hay Associates that the Service commissioned. While improving the reliability of agent judgments will not necessarily lead to increased validity, such an increase in validity is unlikely to occur if the judgments of one agent bear little resemblance to the judgments of another. In this regard, if one could establish the decision rules employed by the "best" agents in making predictions (e.g., the most experienced agents, or those agents whose judgments are most respected by their peers), then at least one could begin to raise the performance level of all agents to that of the "best" agents. Again, it should be clear that this approach does not seek to answer how "good," in terms of validity, the "best" agents actually are.

(4) Some attention might be given to the interventions that are initiated when an agent predicts that a threat exists. A first question might be the integrity of the interventions--that is, the extent to which they are actually carried out as planned. When a family member is requested to stay in contact with a threatening individual while a protected person is visiting the area, for example, does the family member actually do it? How often do the family members "lose" the individual for certain periods during the visit? How often, for that matter, do subjects manage to elude the Secret Service agents surveilling them? One could assess, in this regard, the relative integrity of various modes of surveillance (e.g., family member versus agents).

MEMORANDUM

On Case Management and Decision-Making

Loren H. Roth, M.D., M.P.H.
Director, Law and Psychiatry Program
Western Psychiatric Institute and Clinic
University of Pittsburgh
Pittsburgh, Pennsylvania

I would like to present a somewhat different perspective about the problems of the Secret Service. To put it bluntly, I see Secret Service personnel as having two problems: first (of course) to protect the president; second, to ensure that agent behavior is "reasonable" or "appears reasonable" in relationship to the Secret Service mission. Some problems of the Secret Service agents appear no different than problems confronting emergency room physicians who must evaluate potentially violent persons. The problem is not just "what predictions do we make?" but also "how should we act?" or "what decision rules should we employ with respect to a host of potential next steps to be taken or not taken?"

Assassination attempts and other attempts to harm public officials are extremely rare events. Developing methods of prediction for the most relevant outcomes will be difficult (probably impossible), even utilizing a "proxy" approach. The first goal, protecting the president, requires assessment of the factors that Saleem Shah has nicely identified in his paper (assailants, targets, and situations). Were I a Secret Service agent, I might, however, perceive the problem somewhat differently; for example, how should I act when a threat is brought to my attention? For the Secret Service, the problem is thus not only that of "prediction," but also of planning interventions and adequately monitoring and assessing the threat situation.

The worst fallacy for the Secret Service might be for it to assume that dangerousness is predictable, or to act as if a decision about a subject's dangerousness may be reliably or validly made at a single point in time.

In evaluating potentially dangerous persons in the emergency room, we consider different management strategies and alternatives. Decision rules (to act or not to act) will differ as pertains to (1) the decision to hospitalize voluntarily or involuntarily, (2) notify the police or potential victims, (3) question other persons about the patient (e.g., relatives and friends), (4) obtain other information and records, (5) send the person home under the surveillance of relatives or friends, (6) phone the patient tomorrow, (7) do outreach, and/or (8) follow the person over time.

The base rate for missile attack on Pittsburgh is presently zero. Nevertheless, there is (I hope) a system in place for tracking and monitoring of enemy activity, including a number of decision points wherein certain steps will be taken when a "signal" is detected indicating that missiles are or may be coming. By analogy, clinicians know that preventing future violent behavior, even for high-risk persons, involves continuous monitoring of subjects at risk not only to assess (a) changes in mental state and (b) the provocative value of current situations, but also to (c) continue the "minuet" with the person at risk. We most effectively prevent future violent behavior by adjusting our interventions over time in light of ongoing information and feedback about a person's course—not by making long-term predictions.

I thus suggest that one focus of our meeting should be to discuss and critique the procedures, monitoring efforts, and additionally collected data, that the Secret Service utilizes once a potential assailant is identified.

The Secret Service's problem in protecting the president is not only scientific, but also political. To state this is not to denigrate the problem or to make a cynical comment. It is to emphasize that Secret Service agents face problems that are somewhat similar to problems clinicians face in emergency rooms. Secret Service agents and clinicians must make behavioral interventions, but also must develop and implement monitoring procedures which are reasonable (and which, were tragedy to result, would be judged reasonable) in light of present day knowledge.

It is these "mundane questions" that interest me as much as the more theoretical issues about the prediction of dangerousness. We need to explore questions such as: Under what circumstances might the Secret Service perform two different evaluations by two different agents, rather than having to rely on the judgment of only one agent? What type of background information about subjects is routinely collected, how is it collected, what is its reliability and validity, and how is it used to establish profiles for continuing surveillance? What happens when a "Quarterly Investigation" subject "gets lost" to follow-up?

MEMORANDUM

Secret Service "Dangerousness" Research

Franklin E. Zimring, J.D.
University of Chicago Law School
Chicago, Illinois

This memorandum outlines three research soundings the United
States Secret Service might undertake.  The first two would involve
agency files and field staff follow-up, while the third requires a
prospective experiment comparing the stress interview with
alternative techniques.  These proposals are sketched out in this
form to provoke reactions from other committee members and to inspire
similar preliminary memoranda from my colleagues.

(1) Classification of dangerous subjects:  a proxy validation.

When subjects are brought to the attention of the Service,
initial investigations are conducted to determine whether, and to
what extent, the subject represents a threat to personal security
that falls within the jurisdiction of the Service.  These predictions
of possible dangerousness are a major field activity of the Secret
Service:  surveillance and case closure decisions are based on
initial classifications as well as subsequent events.  Thus, if the
Service screens 100 persons who threaten protected parties, an
important early task is identifying the relatively small number who
are "dangerous."

Obviously, it would be nice to know how effective the Service
is in classifying subjects at present, and what objective criteria
predict jurisdictional danger.  The problem is that overt attempts
against persons within the protective jurisdiction of the Service are
too rare to permit direct validation.  An imperfect alternative,
still worth trying, would be to use five year follow-up data now
collected by the Service to see whether those classified as dangerous
are more likely to engage in events which are plausible "proxies" for
jurisdictional danger.  Two plausible proxies are (1) acts of
interpersonal violence, and (2) suicide, particularly suicide
attempted or committed in obviously attention-getting fashion.  I am
unprepared to argue that these "proxy" behaviors are perfect or even
adequate substitutes for political violence.  However, finding that
the group classified as dangerous is more inclined towards these
behaviors in the five years after coming to the attention of the
Service would be an encouraging indication that current Service
criteria are efficient predictors of overt behavior.  Finding no
difference between groups would be a sobering indication of lack of
linkage between Service criteria and overt behavior during the

follow-up period. Further, this kind of follow-up study can provide associations between objective factors, known at the point of initial investigation, and subsequent overt behavior. Certain factors obviously related to risk, such as whether the individual is at large or under restraint, would have to be controlled in the comparison. And the findings would be far from definitive. But the above study seems like the "least worst" way to approximate a validity study of Service predictions.

(2) Determinants of the volume of threats.

Little is known about what determines the volume of different kinds of threats against political figures over time. Since the Service does not control its own "in box," there may be value in modest explorations of variations in different types of jurisdictional threat over time, seasonal variations, and the extent to which publicized events precipitate increases or decreases in the volume of particular types of threatening gestures. Unlike the proxy validation study suggested above, preliminary soundings on variations over time or with events on the volume of jurisdictional threats could begin as a low cost, in-house activity of the Service. Indeed, some of the basic data may have already been collected for housekeeping or analytic purposes. Exposing social and behavioral science consultants to these preliminary soundings could then lead to more sophisticated designs for collaborative research.

(3) A "stress interview" experiment.

Questions about the stress interview occurred early in Secret Service request for technical assistance. Here there might be room for a random assignment experiment. Given the large numbers of new cases, the question is really how to determine to what extent increasing the "temperature" of an interview increases its informational yield. Randomly assigning all or some classes of Secret Service interviews between stress and non-stress modes might help answer the question. It is possible to find out whether stress interviews increase the initial confidence of the agent. Further, the five year follow-up might tell the Service whether this particular device improves prediction of dangerousness.

National Academy of Sciences

Institute of Medicine Workshop on Behavioral Research and the Secret
Service:  Problems in Assessing and Managing Dangerous Behavior
MARCH 8 - 10, 1981

Invitational Conference Participants

W. Walter Menninger, M.D., Chair  (P) *
Senior Staff Psychiatrist
Division of Law & Psychiatry
Menninger Foundation
Topeka, KS


Elissa P. Benedek, M.D.  (P)
Director
Center for Forensic Psychiatry
Ann Arbor, MI

James H. Billings, Ph.D., M.P.H.
Director
Institute of Epidemiology
   and Behavioral Medicine
San Francisco, CA

Alfred Blumstein, Ph.D.
Professor
School of Urban and
   Public Affairs
Carnegie-Mellon University
Pittsburgh, PA

Sara Eddy, Ed.D.
Assistant Medical Director
McLean/Bridgewater Program
McLean Hospital
Belmont, MA

Hillel Einhorn, Ph.D.
Professor of Behavioral Science
Director
Center for Decision Research
Graduate School of Business
University of Chicago
Chicago, IL

Joseph T. English, M.D.  (P) *
Director of Psychiatry
St. Vincent's Hospital
New York, NY

Robert A. Fein, Ph.D.
Assistant Psychologist
Program Director
McLean/Bridgewater Program
McLean Hospital
Belmont, MA

Shervert H. Frazier, M.D.  (P)
Psychiatrist-in-Chief
McLean Hospital
Belmont, MA

R. Kirkland Gable, Ph.D., J.D.
Associate Professor
Department of Psychology
California Lutheran College
Thousand Oaks, CA

Don M. Gottfredson, Ph.D.
Dean
School of Criminal Justice
Rutgers University
Newark, NJ

(P) = Planning Committee Member
(*) = Member, Institute of Medicine

185

Charles R. Halpern, J.D. *
Associate Professor and Director
Institute for Public Representation
Georgetown University Law Center
Washington, DC

David A. Hamburg, M.D.  (P) *
Director
Division of Health Policy,
   Research and Education
Harvard University
Cambridge, MA

Kenneth R. Hammond, Ph.D.  (P)
Professor of Psychology
Center for Research on Judgment
   and Policy
Institute of Behavioral Sciences
University of Colorado
Boulder, CO

Mr. Brian M. Jenkins
Director
Security and Subnational
   Conflict Program
Rand Corporation
Santa Monica, CA

John R. Lion, M.D.
Professor of Psychiatry
Institute of Psychiatry and
   Human Behavior
Department of Psychiatry
University of Maryland
   School of Medicine
Baltimore, MD

Robert Michels, M.D.
Professor and Chairman
Department of Psychiatry
Cornell University
   Medical College
New York, NY

John Monahan, Ph.D.
Professor of Law and
Professor of Psychology
University of Virginia
   Law School
Charlottesville, VA

Frank M. Ochberg, M.D.  (P)
Director
Department of Mental Health
State of Michigan
Lansing, MI

Loren Roth, M.D., M.P.H.
Director
The Law and Psychiatry Program
   at Western Psychiatric
   Institute and Clinic
University of Pittsburgh
Pittsburgh, PA

Saleem A. Shah, Ph.D.  (P)
Chief
Center for Studies of Crime
   and Delinquency
National Institute of Mental
   Health
Rockville, MD

Honorable Patricia M. Wald
United States Court of Appeals
   for the District of Columbia
   Circuit
United States Court House
Washington, DC

Marguerite Q. Warren, Ph.D.
Professor
School of Criminal Justice
University of New York, Albany
Albany, NY

Charles H. Whitebread, L.L.B.  (P)
Law Professor
Visiting Professor of Law
University of Southern
   California Law Center
University Park
Los Angeles, CA

Marvin E. Wolfgang, Ph.D.  (P)
Professor of Sociology and
   Professor of Law
University of Pennsylvania
Center for Studies in Criminology
   and Criminal Law
Philadelphia, PA

## Secret Service

H. S. Knight
Director
United States Secret Service
Washington, DC

Robert R. Snow
Acting Assistant Director
Office of Protective Research
United States Secret Service
Washington, DC

Edward Walsh
Special Agent-in-Charge
Intelligence Division
United States Secret Service
Washington, DC

Robert Kyanko
Assistant Special
  Agent-in-Charge
Intelligence Division
United States Secret Service
Washington, DC

Dwight T. Colley
Special Agent, Office of
  Training
United States Secret Service
Washington, DC

## Consultants to the United States Secret Service

Lewis R. Goldberg, Ph.D.
Professor of Psychology at
University of Oregon
Institute for Measurement
  of Personality
Eugene, OR

Edwin I. Megargee, Ph.D.
Professor of Psychology
Psychology Department
Florida State University
Tallahassee, FL

## Institute of Medicine

Frederick C. Robbins, M.D.
President
Institute of Medicine
National Academy of Sciences
Washington, DC

Fredric Solomon, M.D.
Director
Division of Mental Health and
  Behavioral Medicine
Institute of Medicine
National Academy of Sciences
Washington, DC

Delores Parron, Ph.D.
Associate Director
Division of Mental Health
  and Behavioral Medicine
National Academy of Sciences
Washington, DC

Jane Takeuchi, Ph.D.
Staff Officer
Division of Mental Health and
  Behavioral Medicine
Institute of Medicine
National Academy of Sciences
Washington, DC

Mireille Mesias
Secretary
Institute of Medicine
National Academy of Sciences
Washington, DC

## Observers

Robert Carvalho, M.D.
Resident in Psychiatry
St. Vincent's Hospital
New York, NY  10011

Bernard Vittone, M.D.
Resident in Psychiatry
St. Vincent's Hospital
New York, NY  10011

National Academy of Sciences
INSTITUTE OF MEDICINE
2101 Constitution Avenue
Washington, D. C.   20418

Invitational Workshop on Behavioral Research and
The Secret Service:  Problems in Assessing
and Managing Dangerous Behavior
March 8 - 10, 1981

W. Walter Menninger, M.D., Chair

Sunday, March 8, 1981

Plenary Session

Watergate Terrace Restaurant, 2650 Virginia Avenue, N. W.

6:30 P.M.          Cocktails

7:00               Dinner

8:00               Opening Remarks and Orientation

                          Frederick C. Robbins, M.D.
                          President, Institute of Medicine

                          W. Walter Menninger, M.D.
                          Menninger Foundation

                          H. S. Knight
                          Director, United States Secret Service

                          David A. Hamburg, M.D.
                          Harvard University

8:30               Introduction of Conferees

8:40               United States Secret Service Presentation:   Two
                      Case Illustrations

                          Edward Walsh
                          Special Agent-in-Charge, Intelligence Division

                               Case #1                (minutes 15)
                               Questions and Discussion    (minutes 20)

                               Case #2                (minutes 15)
                               Questions and Discussion    (minutes 20)

Sunday, March 8, 1981 (continued)

9:50 P.M.          Logistics, Closing Remarks

                   W. Walter Menninger, M.D.

10:05              Adjourn

Monday, March 9, 1981

                   National Academy of Sciences Building, Lecture Room

8:30 A.M.          Coffee, tea, juice

9:00               Charge to the Workshop, Clarification of Format

                   W. Walter Menninger, M.D.

                   United States Secret Service Expectations

                        Robert R. Snow
                        Acting Assistant Director, Office of
                        Protective Research

9:30-10:45         Plenary Presentations and Discussion - Assessment
                             NAS Lecture Room

                   Basic Question:  What can behavioral science offer
                   to assist the U.S.S.S in its task of assessing
                   persons who threaten their protectees (i.e.,
                   potential assassins)?

                   Sub-Question A:  What is the state-of-the-art on
                   the capacity to predict dangerousness or potential
                   assassination?

                        John Monahan, Ph.D.
                        University of Virginia          (15 minutes)

                   Sub-Question B:  Which interview or assessment
                   techniques may be most useful in this task?

                        Shervert H. Frazier, M.D.
                        McLean Hospital, Belmont, MA    (15 minutes)

                   Sub-Question C:  What experiences/findings from
                   parallel activities may be applicable to the
                   U.S.S.S. task?

                        Don M. Gottfredson, Ph.D. (parole prediction)
                        Rutgers University            ( 5 minutes)

190

Monday, March 9, 1981 (continued)

James H. Billings, Ph.D., M.P.H.
(epidemiology)
Pacific Medical Center
San Francisco                          ( 5 minutes)

Brian M. Jenkins (credibility of threats)
Rand Corporation                       ( 5 minutes)

11:00 A.M.      Workshop Sessions:  All participants divide into
                three workshop groups, each to address main issue of
                assessment and specific sub-questions, including
                exploration of:

                        Novel ideas, new approaches
                        Training implications for U.S.S.S.
                        Research needs and opportunities

                Workshop A:     NAS Lecture Room
                Workshop B:     Room 180
                Workshop C:     Room 280

12:15 P.M.      Lunch - NAS Refectory

 1:30           Workshop groups reconvene

 3:00           Coffee-tea-juice Break

 3:30           Plenary Presentations and Discussion - Management
                              NAS Lecture Room

                Basic Question:  What can behavioral science offer to
                assist the U.S.S.S. in its task of managing persons
                deemed to be serious threats to their protectees
                (i.e., potential assassins)?

                Sub-Question A:  What is the present knowledge of
                principal techniques for the management of
                potentially violent persons?

                        W. Walter Menninger, M.D.         (15 minutes)

                Sub-Question B:  What are the difficulties and what
                improvements can be suggested in the relationship
                between the U.S.S.S. and the mental health delivery
                system/institutions/practitioners?

                        Joseph T. English, M.D.
                        St. Vincent's Hospital,
                        New York City                     (15 minutes)

191

Monday, March 9, 1981 (continued)

Discussion from the floor (Sub-Questions A & B)

4:30 P.M.        Sub-Question C: What are the legal, ethical and medical implications of intervention measures?

Roundtable Discussion

Charles R. Halpern, J.D.
Georgetown University Law Center

Robert Michels, M.D.
Cornell University Medical College

Charles H. Whitebread, L.L.B.
University of Southern California Law Center

R. Kirkland Gable, Ed.D., J.D.
California Lutheran College, Thousand Oaks, CA

Discussion from the floor (Sub-Question C)

5:30        Cocktails

6:30        Buffet Dinner - NAS Refectory

7:30        Workshop groups reconvene: Each group to address main issue of management and specific sub-questions, including exploration of:

Novel ideas, new approaches
Training implications
Reseach needs and opportunities

9:30        Adjourn for the day

(Groups chairs, vice-chairs, and workshop staff review the day's activities.)

Tuesday, March 10, 1981

National Academy of Sciences Building, Lecture Room

8:30 A.M.        Coffee, tea, juice

9:00        Workshop groups reconvene: Each group synthesizes previous discussions, highlighting areas of consensus and sharpest division; and makes suggestions concerning promising lines of inquiry, training, and

Tuesday, March 10, 1981 (continued)

> operational aspects of U.S.S.S. procedures in light
> of what behavioral science can contribute. (Includes
> consideration of U.S.S.S. list of questions.)

10:30        Coffee-tea-juice Break

10:45        <u>Plenary Session, NAS Lecture Room</u>

Workshop groups reports and general discussion

12:00        <u>Lunch - NAS Refectory</u>

1:00 P.M.        <u>Plenary Session, NAS Lecture Room</u>

Summary impressions, brief comments, ideas, and/or
suggestions from each conference participant

3:00        U.S.S.S. Response

3:20        Closing Remarks

W. Walter Menninger, M.D.

3:30        Conference adjourns

DATE DUE